MW00568323

Presented To

_____

From

_____

Date

_____

# THE
# POWER *of*
# FORGIVENESS

# THE
# POWER *of*
# FORGIVENESS

## RELEASING GOD'S POWER

## DR. BRIAN ADAMS

© Copyright 2012—Dr. Brian Adams

All rights reserved. This book is protected by the copyright laws of the United States of America. This book may not be copied or reprinted for commercial gain or profit. The use of short quotations or occasional page copying for personal or group study is permitted and encouraged. Permission will be granted upon request. Unless otherwise identified, Scripture quotations are taken from the King James Version. Scripture quotations marked NASB are taken from the NEW AMERICAN STANDARD BIBLE® Copyright © 1960, 1962, 1963, 1968, 1971, 1972, 1973, 1975, 1977, 1995 by the Lockman Foundation. Used by permission. All emphasis within Scripture quotations is the author's own. Please note that Destiny Image's publishing style capitalizes certain pronouns in Scripture that refer to the Father, Son, and Holy Spirit, and may differ from some publishers' styles. Take note that the name satan and related names are not capitalized. We choose not to acknowledge him, even to the point of violating grammatical rules.

DESTINY IMAGE® PUBLISHERS, INC.
P.O. Box 310, Shippensburg, PA 17257-0310
*"Promoting Inspired Lives."*

Burntree Creative contributed to the design of this book cover. Visit them at: www.BurnTree.com.

This book and all other Destiny Image, Revival Press, MercyPlace, Fresh Bread, Destiny Image Fiction, and Treasure House books are available at Christian bookstores and distributors worldwide.

For a U.S. bookstore nearest you, call 1-800-722-6774.
For more information on foreign distributors, call 717-532-3040.
Reach us on the Internet: www.destinyimage.com.

ISBN 13 TP: 978-0-7684-4144-4
ISBN 13 Ebook: 978-0-7684-8819-7

For Worldwide Distribution, Printed in the U.S.A.
1 2 3 4 5 6 7 8 9 10 /15 14 13 12

# DEDICATION

This book is dedicated to the author and finisher of faith and forgiveness, my Heavenly Father. Thank You, Jesus, for distributing forgiveness to me. Thank You, Holy Spirit, for revealing to me this revelation on the power of forgiveness. Thanks to my pastor, David Chisholm, who has always been an example of one to give grace and forgiveness.

To my wife, Karen, for assisting me in prayer and the editing of this book. She truly is a God-sent helpmate.

To all my children and grandchildren. You are awesome.

To my earthly father, the late Richard Adams, who taught me to share my faith. A special thanks to my mother, Irene Adams, for introducing me to the man from Galilee, Jesus Christ.

# ENDORSEMENTS

It never dawned on me the depth and riches of the power of forgiveness until I got this book. Brian Adams has seen his healing ministry go from 30 percent to 80 percent when people got hold of this revelation. Real forgiveness is a major key to God's favor and power.

Sid Roth
Host, *It's Supernatural!*

I have had the pleasure of serving as Dr. Brian Adams' pastor since 1987. I am thrilled that he has released this revelation of the power of forgiveness in book form. I have heard it said that there are "no enduring relationships without the power of forgiveness," and I would have to agree with that statement. I have watched as Brian has lived the pages of this book and can confirm that the healing power of God is released in this revelation. I have witnessed countless miracles in the Rock Churches over the years as Brian has relentlessly labored to bring salvation, healing, and encouragement to the

Body of Christ. Dr. Adams is one of the most faithful, ardent, hardworking servants I know in the Kingdom of God. He lives to see the captives set free, the sick healed, the blind receive their sight, the deaf receive their hearing, and the lame walk. I know you will be blessed as you read the pages of this book. I highly recommend not only the reading of this book, but the ministry of Dr. Brian Adams!

David Chisholm
Doctor of Ministry, Senior Pastor
The Rock Family Worship Centers

Brian Adams has demonstrated through his ministry the power of forgiveness to bring healing, deliverance, and restoration to many. The Lord says, *"Call to Me and I will answer you, and I will tell you great and mighty things, which you do not know"* (Jer. 33:3 NASB). The Hebrew word *mighty* means "inaccessible." What Brian Adams has demonstrated through his book *The Power of Forgiveness* is how to make healing accessible to you. Brian has been a witness to the mighty power of God. He has witnessed the blind see, the deaf hear, the lame walk, and has seen Jesus heal all kinds of sickness and disease. *The Power of Forgiveness* reveals the keys of the Kingdom that will bring restoration, healing, and deliverance to many. The revelations that the Lord has given to Brian produce spiritual, mental, and emotional miracles as well as physical healings. Because of this message, relationships have been reconciled, friendships renewed, broken lives made whole, and marriages healed. When we release others, God, ourselves, and our bodies, it opens the door for us to receive our own healing. The hindrances and blockages have been removed. To those who want to be used by God in a greater way to bring healing to others, Brian offers truths on how to accomplish this. If you are one who loves to see the sick become well, *The Power of Forgiveness* will cause a dramatic increase in the number of healings you will see in your ministry.

Pastor Tony Kemp
Tony Kemp Ministries

I have come to know Pastor Brian Adams over the past few years, and hearing his testimony has always blessed me, because he ministers from a place of a healed and renewed spirit.

His book deals with the root issues of bitterness. When bitterness hardens the heart, it leads individuals to believe that they are under a closed heaven. They don't feel that their prayers or their worship lifestyle is bringing a breakthrough from the Father. They don't feel that Heaven is responding to them and giving them a victory.

As bitterness takes a strong root in the lives of people, they begin to see sickness, disease, phobias, and fear. These are just a few of the things that Brian addresses in-depth in this book.

I know that as you read this book you will name the people toward whom you have unforgiveness and bitterness. You will be freed from all the years that you have been stuck in confinement.

Pastor Brian has seen countless receive their miracle as they release the pain of unforgiveness. I know that as you pray the salvation and healing prayers after you have read this book, you will have your own testimony of the power of forgiveness and wholeness.

Dr. Renny McLean
Global Glory, Inc.

*Faith Moves God, but Forgiveness
Releases His Power*

*Therefore I always exercise and discipline myself [mortifying my body, deadening my carnal affections, bodily appetites, and worldly desires, endeavoring in all respects] to have a clear (unshaken, blameless) conscience, void of offense toward God and toward men.*

Acts 24:16 AMP

# CONTENTS

# PREFACE

As I was coming to the end of a 40-day fast, I was in prayer. The Lord spoke to me the following statement: *Faith moves Me, but forgiveness releases My power.*

This one line statement from the Holy Spirit was a supernatural seed that immediately began to take root and grow in my spirit. It automatically began to unfold and grow into such a revelation that since then we have seen men, women, and children alike saved, healed, and delivered. All by this very power released when we forgive.

I stand in awe and amazement and give all the glory to the Lord for the thousands of healings and miracles all around the world that have taken place with the preaching of this nugget of faith.

I pray as you read this book, you too will receive your breakthrough, whether it be healing for your body, mind, or bruised soul. May total healing come to you and your entire family.

# INTRODUCTION

How the angelic host of Heaven must have stood in awe as they watched the splendor of creation unfold before their very eyes—seeing planets, stars, black holes, entire universes, all entirely expose the wisdom, the beauty, and the majesty of the Heavenly Father. Surveying the perfection and beauty of the earth, the mountains, streams, oceans, animals, and finally man, sculptured by the very hand of God. Observing a creation that He had formed to love Him, fellowship with Him, adore and worship Him. All this now hurled into chaos, confusion, and planetary misalignment. They were witnessing universal oppression, such as had never been seen before.

The angels now must have wondered how even the Creator would turn this all around. Dominion and authority which had been given this man creature now were in the hands of a former friend, now foe, of Heaven, lucifer. Craftily, He had injected into this perfection of creation the seed of deceit and disobedience that had been birthed in the womb of his own heart years before. Ezekiel 28:15 says, *"Thou wast perfect in thy ways from the day that thou wast created, till iniquity was found in thee."* Here we see the birthing place of sin, the infectious seed which brought about all of this separation.

We read in Genesis how God the Father held court in the Garden that day and judged man, woman, and the serpent. To some this might have seemed harsh, driving the inhabitants by flaming swords out of Eden. Thus began the unfolding tale of a miracle which satan fought tooth and nail, only to once again fail and remain the lesser.

The Scripture tells us that Christ was crucified before the foundation of the earth. Here we see that before man was created, before earth itself was formed, God held as a mystery—the hidden key of His greatest power which in the fullness of time He would release in the substitution of His Son's death and resurrection. How would this galactic catastrophe be reversed? The Creator would release to humankind—*forgiveness!*

God's supernatural release of His greatest power was birthed out of His love—He would forgive them. *Faith moves God, but forgiveness releases His power.* One cannot be in harmony with the Creator without having received forgiveness. It is there for the asking; simply ask and receive. He is making this antidote—this remedy to the disastrous plague called sin—available to all.

He has commissioned ambassadors to travel to the four corners of this earth and establish everywhere a Kingdom station, which in a sense is a clinic to make available the vaccination of reconciliation to the Father. This sin disease miracle antidote purchased by the Son's blood can take away this second death-causing disease and instill an immune system which will allow eternal life to the subject who repents of his or her sins and accepts this gift of salvation. God has forgiven us. Will humankind heed the serious call from Heaven to once again walk in His original purpose, being a son? We are called to bring forth righteous seeds and train generations to worship and honor the Lord our God.

*Chapter 1*

# In the Beginning

I had grown up with a loving Christian mother who taught me all of the Bible stories and explained to a certain degree the need for Jesus. Through the emotional vehicle called puberty, satan began to drive me into a land of self-gratification, experimenting with many of the things this world had to offer.

Little did I know that once the door to sin had been opened, a spiritual vacuum would begin to pull me farther into darkness until I felt there was no hope at all. I had tried everything from aspirin to rock heroin, wine to whisky, and sexual exploits I choose not to explain in detail. I brought shame to my family name as a drunk, drug dealer, thief, and con artist. I had sunk so low that the only out I saw was to end my life.

I'll never forget the day I went on a hill to communicate to God before killing myself. I called on His name and He introduced me to the awesome manifestation of His grace that I had never known—a grace called forgiveness.

I know it was God who wooed me upon that hill; He knew that when I called on Him, it would set me off on the road to my destiny.

*And it shall come to pass, that whosoever shall call on the name of the Lord shall be saved* (Acts 2:21).

Drugs, alcohol, and sex were not my problem. It was sin. I was separated from God, having no relationship with Him. I had a sin problem. I needed to be born again. God the Father that day released from Heaven forgiveness purchased at Calvary by Christ's blood for Brian Adams. Being forgiven now by God, He opened the door to the power of restoration and renewal. Another man had been freed from the bondage of slavery to sin. Oh the rejoicing that took place before the angels that day in Heaven! (See Luke 15:10.)

Once forgiveness was imparted to me, supernatural power from Heaven through the Holy Ghost began to do miracles in my life.

I was now born again. I was saved. Old things of the past were dead and gone. I was a new creature in Christ, something that never existed before.

*Therefore, if any man be in Christ, he is a new creature: old things are passed away; behold, all things are become new* (2 Corinthians 5:17).

A new wine skin was just waiting to be filled with a new wine from Heaven.

*And He spake also a parable unto them; No man putteth a piece of a new garment upon an old; if otherwise, then both the new maketh a rent, and the piece that was taken out*

*of the new agreeth not with the old. And no man putteth
new wine into old bottles; else the new wine will burst the
bottles, and be spilled, and the bottles shall perish. But new
wine must be put into new bottles; and both are preserved.
No man also having drunk old wine straightway desireth
new: for he saith, The old is better* (Luke 5:36-39).

I was supernaturally translated from the kingdom of darkness to God's light.

*Who hath delivered us from the power of darkness, and
hath translated us into the kingdom of His dear Son*
(Colossians 1:13).

I know it sounds kind of sci-fi, almost like, "Beam me
up, Scotty." Until you have experienced it, there isn't really
an explanation. It truly is supernatural. It's where God takes
His super and touches your natural.

- Things looked brighter through my eyes.
- Sadness and depression were gone.
- Hope and happiness which hadn't been there since
  early childhood had returned.

I didn't in any way deserve what I received that day. It
was a beginner's class to grace and forgiveness. It truly was
a gift and no works could purchase what had happened to
me. I had been forgiven much. Now I was about to start my
walk with the Lord.

*Wherefore I say unto thee, Her sins, which are many, are
forgiven; for she loved much: but to whom little is forgiven, the same loveth little* (Luke 7:47).

I had lived so many years drunk, drug-addled, and in the realm of darkness. Now my addictions, uncontrollable fleshly lusts, and fears were gone. My mind was quieter than I can even remember. This peace that I was experiencing flooded my soul. His love drowned my fears, and for the first time I began to realize that just maybe there was a purpose for me. The street life I had been living required payment for wrongdoing. A person had to make a wrong somehow right. Oh, this was a debt you had to pay and the worse the offense, the greater the debt.

Our carnal minds even had some offenses, like murder, rape, adultery, etc. that you couldn't be forgiven. To forgive appeared to be a sign of weakness and to some even to forgive would mean that the offender wasn't wrong. Our natural minds can't understand that to forgive is actually one of the most powerful acts a human can do. It makes them walk in the supernatural, the God realm. So many people think that to become born again means that you become perfect. That's not what it means. It simply means you've been forgiven. You've received forgiveness from the Lord and now His power has been loosed to you, through you, and on you. You actually become a new person in Christ; and just like a child, you have to be taught to walk, talk, and think this new God-life.

Entering into His Kingdom is like entering into another country. You don't understand the customs, language, or laws. The kingdom of darkness and the Kingdom of God's Son are as different as day and night. In the following chapters you will find out that in God's Kingdom we have received forgiveness and therefore we are supposed to become agents, so to speak, of distribution of this power of forgiveness.

All through this book you will see this phrase, *"Faith moves God, but forgiveness releases His power."* His power is His Spirit, His Spirit is called the anointing, and His anointing is what sets you free.

> *And it shall come to pass in that day, that his burden shall be taken away from off thy shoulder, and his yoke from off thy neck, and the yoke shall be destroyed because of the anointing* (Isaiah 10:27).

People are captive and in bondage because of decisions they have made. The actions that follow those decisions open doors to the enemy. Once he has built a stronghold, there is no escaping unless we repent and enter into God's presence, and then we receive forgiveness which releases His power/anointing. His anointing released destroys the strongholds built by the devil.

> *When a strong man armed keepeth his palace, his goods are in peace: But when a stronger than he shall come upon him, and overcome him, he taketh from him all his armour wherein he trusted, and divideth his spoils* (Luke 11:21-22).

## Anointed to Restore

I have found out in these 25 years of walking with the Lord that the greatest anointing of God is the anointing of forgiveness and then restoration. The Word of God tells us that we humans think totally different from God. We don't understand Him or His ways.

*But the natural man receiveth not the things of the Spirit of God: for they are foolishness unto him: neither can he know them, because they are spiritually discerned* (1 Corinthians 2:14).

It actually takes the Lord opening an understanding of the Word in order for us to understand. *"Then opened He their understanding, that they might understand the scriptures"* (Luke 24:45).

I pray now in Jesus' name that the Lord Jesus Christ would open up your understanding of the Scriptures and His will that you would forgive and then receive His forgiveness in every area of your life. We must forgive others, ourselves, and even God Himself, no matter how little or how big the offense. I pray you let it go and release it and the past. Many people make the statement, "I forgive, but I won't forget." You might have even said that yourself. You and I both know that's not right.

Human love has conditions. You have to perform, meet certain standards, and pay back debts. God's love is unconditional. It forgives, releases from debt, and remembers no more. The Bible tells us that when God forgives us, He also separates our sin from us as far as the East is from the West. We also need to forgive and separate the offense from the person. It may take many times of reminding ourselves that we have made a decision to forgive and release the individual from his or her debt against us. We have to take our thoughts captive daily. Daily take up our cross and follow Him.

God forgave us for Christ's sake while we were still sinners. Let me say it this way. While we were still wrong and unable to pay our debt which would release us from our prison of sin, He paid a debt He didn't owe. We owed a debt we couldn't pay. Praise God! He did this for you and me. Have you received your gift of forgiveness? If you have received your forgiveness free from God, why are you trying to charge others for theirs?

In this Kingdom there are different rules, regulations, and principles we must live by. We must allow ourselves to become converted to God's way of living, thinking, and behaving. He wants to teach us to play well with others, so to speak. I remember someone once said, "Can't we all just get along?"

Remember, the devil subtracts by division. He lies, steals, and kills.

*The thief cometh not, but for to steal, and to kill, and to destroy: I am come that they might have life, and that they might have it more abundantly* (John 10:10).

He wants you to become a covenant-breaker like him. If you get infected with unforgiveness, you will be tormented and walk in hate. Bitterness, sickness, and infirmity will take control in relationships, marriages, and so on.

Make a decision to be open-minded and allow the Holy Ghost to reveal to you the power of God that can be released through forgiveness. *Faith moves God, but forgiveness releases His Power.*

Over the years I have seen people excuse their walking in unforgiveness, anger, or even rage. They blame their culture or their race. They blame what happened years before they were even born. I have Irish in my bloodline. I could say, "Well, you know, the Irish have a temper." Just use it as an excuse for my outburst of anger and never deal with it.

In the Spirit, there is no male or female, Jew or Greek, white, brown, or black. God's Word, if read and applied, will take away all your excuses, claims, or any rights to hold on to your unforgiveness.

Unforgiveness is sin. John the Baptist preached, *"Repent ye: for the kingdom of heaven is at hand"* (Matt. 3:2). Unforgiveness:

- Blocks healing
- Blocks you from being forgiven
- Hinders prayers being answered
- Hinders your offering being accepted by God
- Opens doors to the devil to oppress you
- Releases the tormenting spirits upon your body and mind.

For Christ's sake, repent, forgive, and receive forgiveness and total deliverance.

## Unforgiveness Blocks Healing

The same Spirit who forgives also heals. So if the Word tells us that if we don't forgive, we can't be forgiven, then if we don't forgive, we can't be healed. I have seen hundreds of people who said they had been prayed for so many times without results and then we prayed and forgave people from their past. Now these were people who they thought they had already forgiven. It appears they had forgiven with their lips, but not with their hearts. They would begin to cry, repent, forgive, and release the people from having to make things right before they would forgive them.

Remember that when God has forgiven us, all is taken away, separated from us as far as East from West. It takes God's love to do this. They will know we are Christians by our love. The fruit of God's love is to forgive. Once they truly forgave, we prayed again for healing, and they were healed in Jesus' Name. We can know to do right and even practice right principles, but practicing right principles apart from God isn't sufficient. His Word tells us, *"...Not by might, nor by power, but by My Spirit, saith the Lord of hosts"* (Zech. 4:6).

If we could save ourselves, there would have been no need for Christ to die on Calvary. No death, no resurrection, no repentance to Him. We know this isn't so, and that we need the blood of Jesus. There is no remission of sin without the shedding of blood. We must become born again to enter the Kingdom. To become born again takes a supernatural act of God's power. God's power is released when true, godly repentance happens. *Faith moves God, but forgiveness releases His power.*

The state that man is in before being born again is a state of spiritual death—eternal separation from God. Demonic yokes hold us in bondage. The spirit of this world has us blinded so we can't see our need for help. Forgiveness releases God's power, which is His Holy Spirit, which is His anointing, which is the only yoke-destroying power on earth. We need God. We were created to be forgiven and have fellowship with Him. We were created to have fellowship with one another. The devil subtracts by division. He brings offense, bitterness, and hatred in marriages, between brothers and sisters, between cultures, races, and nations.

Sin is devastating. One man's sin (Adam) brought death into the world, both physical and spiritual. The wages of sin is death. How much devastation has all the sin of people since then continued to bring into the world? All of our righteousness is as filthy rags. All have sinned and fallen short of the glory of God. True righteousness from Him can only be imputed by faith, and only after we have been forgiven.

There's an old song we used to sing and it went something like this, "Open the eyes of my heart, Lord." Truly every man, woman, and child needs to have their eyes open to the condition of their hearts. Not only lost people, but people who have become born again then fallen into unforgiveness. Remember if you don't forgive, you won't be forgiven. Let's say you become born again. All is going great for the first couple of years. Then someone offends you. You now have unforgiveness toward this person. Twenty years go by and you just have blanked this offense out of your mind. Now for twenty years every time you've sinned or messed up and asked for forgiveness and prayed First John 1:9, you haven't been forgiven because you never dealt with that old offense. You think you are right with God, but sickness and infirmity and double-mindedness rule in your life.

You get prayer and it doesn't seem to work. You eventually quit praying and only seek man's help through medicine and counseling. Your faith now is in the natural realm and in yourself. You no longer look to God and don't even realize what has happened.

If you stay in the Church, it is just out of a religious habit. You no longer witness or invite people to church, and there's no happiness in your heart. A dark cloud of depression covers you and follows wherever you go. Instead of bringing life and joy, you reproduce darkness and depression. The devil has you right where he wants you. You become a powerless believer who actually doesn't believe anymore. It's like satan took a remote and placed you on pause.

You're miserable, tormented by spirits of infirmity, depression, and fear. There is only one way out: It is to forgive the people who have wronged you—not only forgive but release them from any obligation to make their wrong right. This is God's way, and when you do, the devil's legal right to oppress you is gone. You now can receive the power of God and be set free in Jesus' Name.

I believe that after reading this book, if you will do what God has shown me, you can and will be forgiven, healed, and set free in your body, soul, and spirit. I release my faith in God for you to be forgiven and for the power of God to be released in and on your life.

After receiving this revelation from Heaven, I first put it to use in my life. I then began to share it with others and have actually seen hundreds, if not thousands, set free by the power of God. I've shared this message in Africa,

Nicaragua, Costa Rica, Honduras, and on multiple Indian reservations. I have preached this message on forgiveness all across America and on television programs that have reached into millions of homes. One of our programs is currently airing in Karachi, Pakistan. Muslim and Hindu people are being set free by God's power. Thank You, Jesus. I believe if I am faithful to continue to share this message, many doors will be opened.

I've learned over the years that we have our personal relationship with the Lord, as well as a corporate relationship we have with the Body of Christ. The devil tries not only to cause problems in the church, but in our personal relationship with God. I have met and prayed with hundreds of people over the years who are mad at God for various reasons—the death of a loved one, unanswered prayers, unsaved family, and broken marriages are only a few I can mention. A lot of times God gets blamed for our mistakes. We must not forget what the Scriptures tell us: *"Be not deceived; God is not mocked: for whatsoever a man soweth, that shall he also reap"* (Gal. 6:7).

If we don't forgive, we can't be forgiven. We can't be healed. We can't be delivered. It also hinders our prayer life and our worship life. It even attacks our offerings and financial life.

## Love, Not Performance

I will never forget the day my wife came home from a training class that she attended for her employer. She began to explain to me a comment the instructor had made. This one line has helped change my life. This seminar was on stress management. She shared this statement: "Lower your expectations of people and your stress level will go down." This doesn't mean you lower your moral standards and all expectations of yourself or other people around you. But quit expecting them to perform to the high level you have set for everyone. When people don't perform or act according to how we expect them to act, we get offended. We then step into the "performance syndrome." You do things my way or I am taking my bat and glove home. You remember that kid on the block now, don't you?

In order to forgive and let go, we need to lower our expectations. We need to give to people the same grace and forgiveness and patience we want to receive from God ourselves. So many of the world's problems, I believe, can be solved if we would obey the Word of God. He tells us to love and forgive. He knows that our walking in unforgiveness is simply a death trap used by the devil to hinder us and stop us from our Kingdom call. He knows the devil will use this to open the door to torment us night and day, day and night.

When the giant was challenging the army of Israel, he would come out early in the morning and make his threats and bring fear (torment) upon these soldiers so that they would start their day in fear and torment, ruining their day. Then he would come out just before dark and challenge again. This way their nights would be tormented also. They would lose sleep and be afraid, wearing them down night and day (see 1 Sam. 17:16).

The enemy wants to deprive us of sleep and get us to eat badly. He wants us to walk in fear, anxiety, anger, and wrath. He knows we were created to walk in love, peace, and righteousness. His tactic is to get our immune system off and our souls and bodies weak. By doing this we are filled with fear instead of faith. Without faith we cannot be in the Spirit. Walking in the Spirit is the only way we can escape fulfilling the lust of the flesh.

We are born with a sinful nature, so we can only expect sinners to sin. We are born this way because of Adam's sin. The devil wants to keep us this way, but Christ died so we could be born again. If we are redeemed by the blood of the Lamb, the price has been paid. We can be free from slavery from sin. If the devil can keep us mad, sad, and depressed, he is getting us back into a sinful nature. Repent and walk in the Spirit.

Not only can we do this, but we have been empowered to do this. When we were saved, we received forgiveness. I believe we received more than what we needed. Use your excess to forgive others. Don't allow yourself to become blinded and deceived by the devil.

Allow love and forgiveness to open your eyes to see the great harvest that lies before us. We all can have a part if we will receive and give forgiveness.

Wait a minute! I came to the end of the first chapter and I haven't given you some definitions of the words *forgive*, *forgiven*, and *forgiving*. If I am going to teach you on something, I want you to be on the same page with me so to speak.

Forgive (according to the American Heritage Dictionary and Collins English Dictionary) means:

- To excuse for a fault or an offense, pardon
- To renounce anger or resentment against
- To absolve from payment of (a debt, for example)
- To refrain from imposing punishment on an offender or demand satisfaction for an offense
- To grant pardon without harboring resentment. *Pardon* more strongly implies release from the liability for a penalty entailed by an offense. To excuse is to pass over a mistake (a fault) without demanding punishment or redress.
- To cease to blame or hold resentment against
- To free from the obligation of
- Stop blaming
- Excuse or overlook
- Bear no malice toward, no longer hold against

*Faith moves God, but forgiveness releases His power.*

# Chapter 2

# BLINDED BY THE FIGHT

Satan is now expelled from Heaven, and dominion has been stolen from humanity on earth. The echo of God's voice saying creation was good seems to have faded so long ago. So much has happened since then, and in the natural it appears to be hopeless with no cure in sight.

When it appears satan has the upper hand in the natural, I want to assure you that God is in control, and on the scene in the unseen. There is more working for you than against you.

The beginning stages to becoming a successful son or daughter in the Kingdom is to become educated in the ways of God and also in the ways spirits work against us. Through many hours in prayer lines and in counseling sessions, I have found that people want to obey God's Word and forgive, but they say people's actions are inexcusable. It was premeditated.

I will start by making this statement. Whatever people perceive is their reality. What this means is simply that no matter how wrong the things that people do or say are, the decision made in the head will be justified in the heart. The enemy will blind people and then use them as puppets. People become the puppets, and the devil is the puppet master. If they think you said or meant something a certain way, then that will trigger them to do what they do. You may not have even done it or said it. You may not have even been in town when it happened. False accusations are one of satan's favorite weapons.

People take their perceptions for reality, even when mistaken, and they will make decisions from their reality even though their perceptions are warped. If people knew they were deceived, then they would not be deceived. Satan has blinded people of the world so they will not see why they need Christ, the Church, the Word, or anything from Heaven.

*...The god of this world hath blinded the minds of them which believe not, lest the light of the glorious gospel of Christ, who is the image of God, should shine unto them* (2 Corinthians 4:4).

We act so surprised when someone close to us does something to hurt us. Who do you expect to hurt you? Someone far away? Someone you don't know? The enemy wants to use people you trust and know so he can get in close enough to hurt you. I hope that in reading this book you will be informed, educated, and inspired to forgive and request forgiveness from God on their behalf. These offenses, these tribulations that come against you are what the apostle Paul calls fiery darts. We are supposed to use our shield of faith to quench, put out, and not let them do damage. We are to expect and pray for the best, be prepared to handle the worst, and always rejoice in our brothers' and sisters' victories.

People in the Church and outside it have been affected much by this cosmic fight between God the Father and two thirds of the angels and satan and his one third. Satan was ejected from Heaven. We see in this next Scripture exactly what happened to lucifer.

*And He said unto them, I beheld Satan as lightning fall from heaven. Behold, I give unto you power to tread on serpents and scorpions, and over all the power of the enemy: and nothing shall by any means hurt you* (Luke 10:18-19).

He then came down on earth to continue his war against God the Father by attacking His children. We must learn that Christ defeated the devil at Calvary and then gave us authority and power over him. We now have power over him, but if we think it is people messing with us then we won't fight the devil in the spirit.

Let's read verse 19 again. *"Behold, I give unto you power to tread on serpents and scorpions, and over all the power of the enemy: and nothing shall by any means hurt you."* It is easier said than done, easier preached than walked, to forgive and to then pray for people. I pray for you to have your eyes opened to the wiles of the devil against you, and to see and find in the Scripture the authority and power the Lord has given us.

Our whole commission is to go preach Christ cruci-fied and resurrected and harvest souls for God's Kingdom. Offenses and unforgivenesses are hindrances to stop us from fulfilling that commission. I have seen so many anointed people fall, backslide, and be taken out of the race because they got mired in unforgiveness.

*For we wrestle not against flesh and blood, but against principalities, against powers, against the rulers of the darkness of this world, against spiritual wickedness in high places* (Ephesians 6:12).

We see here who our true enemy is. Yes, they use us against one another, one offense against another. Our only defense is knowledge of this fact and then the cure is imme-diately forgiving from the cross. Let there be no time for offense to take root.

Now that your eyes are being opened to this arena of spiritual warfare, do not only be ready to forgive, but be vigilant that you are not blinded again and used as a pup-pet in this battle against one another. My faith is that people will get free reading this book and then set others free. Yes, people are being manipulated, but we now have learned to forgive them and have this mindset that they don't know what they are doing. Your offenses came to you as demonic warfare to take your eyes off of your call and your purpose. If people truly believe that they are sons and daughters of God and we are called to work together and guard ourselves from being used by the devil, things will begin to work better in the Kingdom. Let's together spread this revelation of love, laughter, and forgiveness, and we shall soon see the devil defeated in the lives of our family and friends.

There are other fuels the devil uses, such as hatred against races, cultures, economic classes, setting the rich against the poor, or the educated against the uneducated. There is an old saying, "You can't see the forest for the trees." When you become involved in a matter personally you can be blinded by your emotional involvement.

A woman can have a bad relationship with a man and not only have unforgiveness toward that individual, but also begin to hate men and operate in unforgiveness toward all men. Now this can also happen to a man who has been in a bad relationship with a woman. No matter what the object of our hate and unforgiveness is, if we don't deal with it and repent, we will end up blinded by the fight and spend this life in bondage to the tormentors. We finish in a position of having failed to fulfill the call of God in our lives.

## Divine Assignments

There are a certain number of souls attached to everyone's calling. The devil not only wants to torment God's children in an effort to try to get back at God, but he wants to rob us of our identity and keep us bound up. If we are looking through eyes of hurt and unforgiveness, we fail to see the assignment from Heaven on our lives. Souls, souls, souls! I sure am glad that someone completed their assignment on me. What assignment? I'm so glad you asked.

I believe we all are assigned to pray, witness, and intercede on behalf of people. Someone was assigned to pray, fast, and share God's love, Word, and power with me. Just like others, my eyes were blinded. God had special people who loved me enough to stand in the gap and intercede for me, remit my sins, and then request God to forgive me because I truly didn't know what I was doing. I thank God for those people. I thank God for forgiveness.

Distracted, hurt, and abused, we aren't much help to the Kingdom. Once we are hurt, we will be more likely to hurt people than help them. The Scripture tells us, *"A little leaven leaveneth the whole lump"* (Gal 5:9). Once our attitude is wrong and we become blinded to our identity, purpose, and calling, we will spread the blindness.

The devil, being invisible, so cleverly makes us believe it is the people causing us all the problems. Jesus had spiritual insight, discernment, and even said, *"Father, forgive them; for they know not what they do"* (Luke 23:34). Meanwhile, we are sitting in our self-pity crying about how could someone who says they love me do this to me.

Pity, hurt, and pain of rejection weaken us and cause us to withdraw into the cave of the flesh. They successfully keep us from walking in the Spirit of God. If we handle life separated from the Spirit, then we will always be blinded.

"Blinded by the light" was Paul's cry on the road to Damascus. He was blinded from doing things wrong. He turned to Christ. We, however, become "blinded by the fight." The very fiery darts we are supposed to be quenching by our shield of faith have successfully blinded us to enter into warfare of flesh against flesh.

*For we wrestle not against flesh and blood, but against principalities, against powers, against the rulers of the darkness of this world, against spiritual wickedness in high places* (Ephesians 6:12).

*He that saith he is in the light, and hateth his brother, is in darkness even until now. He that loveth his brother abideth in the light, and there is none occasion of stumbling in him. But he that hateth his brother is in darkness, and walketh in darkness, and knoweth not whither he goeth, because that darkness hath blinded his eyes* (1 John 2:9-11).

How many times do we have to be reminded that we don't fight against flesh and blood? We, according to the Bible, fight demonic spirits.

The trap we fall into when we become blinded by hate and unforgiveness is that everyone influences somebody. Many times there are those who have a wide area of influence. We end up with the blind leading the blind.

When darkness blinds us, we meditate and become what we see. Remember, the eye is the window to our souls. If we are spiritually and soulishly blind, then darkness will fill our hearts.

When what we see and feel is what we think, then ultimately we become what we say. We are called to be priests of God. Yes, all of us are called to pray, decree blessings, and share the Gospel of forgiveness. When darkness is blinding us, our words become demonic, and instead of blessing we speak curses. We become distributors of death instead of light.

*"Death and life are in the power of the tongue: and they that love it shall eat the fruit thereof"* (Prov. 18:21). This Scripture again confirms that our words are seeds, and they will grow and bring us a harvest. Fruit will come, positive or negative. What we sow comes back on us. The devil understands how the spirit realm and the natural realm work. That's why he does what he does. He wants you to sow to the carnal. He wants you to sin. Here's what happens when you sin: *"Be not deceived; God is not mocked: for whatsoever a man soweth, that shall he also reap"* (Gal. 6:7). The enemy wants you to speak negative, hateful, unforgiving words, and for your actions to follow those words so you will reap it back.

## It's All About Jesus

Read the next verse to see another spiritual principle.

*For he that soweth to his flesh shall of the flesh reap corruption; but he that soweth to the Spirit shall of the Spirit reap life everlasting* (Galatians 6:8).

Do you remember when Peter was walking on the water? He did fine as long as he kept his eye on Jesus, but the storm caused him to lose focus. The storms the enemy causes blind us to our purpose—our reason for existence. We get our eyes off of Jesus and onto ourselves. The minute we become selfish and our eyes are only on ourselves, we become blinded by the fight.

I don't know any other way to say it, but it's not about us. We need to get all hate, bitterness, envy, and strife out of our lives and allow all the love of God to be shed abroad in our hearts.

Division, strife, hatred, and unforgiveness are smoke screens the devil uses to get us to lose focus on what should be our number one priority, the Great Commission. If we are not walking in a supernatural love toward our brothers and sisters, then the ability to sacrifice our lives and take up the cross to declare the Gospel of forgiveness is impossible. Our fallen nature is selfish. We here in the United States will focus on the American dream when instead we should be focused on Kingdom building and saving lost souls through the message of forgiving, forgetting, and loving.

The Word tells us anything that is not faith is sin (see Rom. 14:23). Romans 6:23 says, *"For the wages of sin is death; but the gift of God is eternal life through Jesus Christ our Lord."* Yes, there truly is a battle between Heaven and earth, between good and evil. The natural realm fights against the spiritual. When we are not sure who the enemy is, the Church experiences what's called friendly fire. Hundreds and even thousands are hurt in churches, offended by their brothers and sisters, husbands and wives.

Sadly, it has become an endless cycle passed from one generation to the next. People are leaving the church hurt, sad, and hating, filled with unforgiveness, becoming blinded in this eternal fight for souls. Hurt people hurt people, abused people abuse people, and molested people molest people. It continues because it is the only way spirits can reproduce themselves to others. They cause a traumatic situation which causes hatred and unforgiveness, and victims are blinded to the truth. Wandering in the darkness, they are fair game to satan to oppress and torment with fears, phobias, and eventually death.

They say when a person is blind that other senses become keener. Maybe this is true in the natural, but in the spiritual, people's ears are deafened to God. Their hearts are hardened, and they continue to be blind to God's way of healing and restoration.

What is it, you ask? *Faith moves God, but forgiveness releases His power!* Forgiveness is one of the keys to the Kingdom. It will unlock the chains that hold the oppressed and tormented and set them free. We need to forgive everyone who has hurt or offended us, forgive ourselves for failures and wrong decisions, and even forgive God if we have anything against Him. Then we can stand before God and ask Him to forgive us. We have sowed forgiveness, released our past, and now when God gives us forgiveness, His power is released to deliver, heal, save, and set the captive free.

By now you must agree that we are in a war. I pray that what you are learning in this book is beginning to teach you the wiles of the devil. These teachings reveal his methods and madness. He hates anyone who has the capability to become sons and daughters of God. He hates that he was defeated and that authority has once again been given to humankind. Jesus called us the light of the world shining in the darkness (see Matt. 5:14). We see and know that satan has blinded people's eyes by getting them to hate and harbor unforgiveness. Now our job is to pray for these people that the god of this world would have his chains broken off of them, and that their eyes would see and ears would hear.

Let's begin to intercede and ask God to forgive them, for they know not what they are doing. They are blinded and stumbling in darkness. When the apostle Paul had his knockdown experience with Jesus on the road to Damascus, He told him that He was sending him to be an eye-opener.

> *But rise, and stand upon thy feet: for I have appeared unto thee for this purpose, to make thee a minister and a witness both of these things which thou hast seen, and of those things in the which I will appear unto thee; delivering thee from the people, and from the Gentiles, unto whom now I send thee, to open their eyes, and to turn them from darkness to light, and from the power of Satan unto God, that they may receive forgiveness of sins, and inheritance among them which are sanctified by faith that is in Me* (Acts 26:16-18).

The whole purpose is to get the people out from under the devil's power and into God's power and light so that forgiveness of sins can be given. Then God's power can be released to do the greatest miracle of changing a sinner to a saint.

Remember, we are needed to network with Heaven and become distributors of forgiveness. I have found that there must be a lot of prayer going up, requesting and interceding, before people are going to be saved. Let's keep praying for God to forgive people. Let's look at the prayer Paul prayed in Ephesians.

> *That the God of our Lord Jesus Christ, the Father of glory, may give unto you the spirit of wisdom and revelation in the knowledge of Him: the eyes of your understanding being enlightened; that ye may know what is the hope of His calling, and what the riches of the glory of His inheritance*

*in the saints, and what is the exceeding greatness of His power to us-ward who believe, according to the working of His mighty power, which He wrought in Christ, when He raised Him from the dead, and set Him at his own right hand in the heavenly places, far above all principality, and power, and might, and dominion, and every name that is named, not only in this world, but also in that which is to come: and hath put all things under His feet, and gave Him to be the head over all things to the church, which is His body, the fulness of Him that filleth all in all* (Ephesians 1:17-23).

I remember a song we used to sing called "Open the Eyes of My Heart, Lord." The words were, "Open the eyes of my heart, Lord. I want to see You." The Bible tells us that when we see Him, we will be like Him (see 1 John 3:2). I pray for that day.

# Be Prepared

I don't know where we get the idea that because we are in the Body of Christ everything is supposed to be OK and there will be no problems. We plainly see that those who served Him were beaten, placed in prison, thrown into a hole, thrown into fiery furnaces and lion's dens, shipwrecked, and more. If any of these things happened today we would be offended at our church leaders and at God. This is exactly how the devil gets us offended, bitter, filled with hatred, and eventually blinded, now doing the Body no good and positioning ourselves and our family in an atmosphere of torment and confession.

What does the Bible say about being done wrong? First Corinthians reads:

*Dare any of you, having a matter against another, go to law before the unjust, and not before the saints? Do ye not know that the saints shall judge the world? and if the world shall be judged by you, are ye unworthy to judge the smallest matters? Know ye not that we shall judge angels? how much more things that pertain to this life? If then ye have judgments of things pertaining to this life, set them to judge who are least esteemed in the church. I speak to your shame. Is it so, that there is not a wise man among you? no, not one that shall be able to judge between his brethren? But brother goeth to law with brother, and that before the unbelievers. Now therefore there is utterly a fault among you, because ye go to law one with another. Why do ye not rather take wrong? why do ye not rather suffer yourselves to be defrauded? Nay, ye do wrong, and defraud, and that your brethren* (1 Corinthians 6:1-8).

It sounds to me by this Scripture that in order to fulfill the Word of God, we need the supernatural love of God to distribute forgiveness and continue to ask and receive forgiveness. The Word of God has more to say about the right way to respond so that we don't become blinded in the fight.

*Bless them which persecute you: bless, and curse not. Rejoice with them that do rejoice, and weep with them that weep. Be of the same mind one toward another. Mind not high things, but condescend to men of low estate. Be not wise in your own conceits. Recompense to no man evil for evil. Provide things honest in the sight of all men. If*

*it be possible, as much as lieth in you, live peaceably with
all men. Dearly beloved, avenge not yourselves, but rather
give place unto wrath: for it is written, Vengeance is mine;
I will repay, saith the Lord. Therefore if thine enemy hunger, feed him; if he thirst, give him drink: for in so doing
thou shalt heap coals of fire on his head. Be not overcome
of evil, but overcome evil with good* (Romans 12:14-21).

That's right, everything that our normal mind tells us, we
are to do the opposite. If we don't read and study to show
ourselves approved unto God, then we will not know how
to properly respond to the storms and offenses that come
against us.

If we are truly dead in Christ, then it makes sense that a
dead man can't get offended. If we walk around with a chip
on our shoulder, we will do the Kingdom more harm than
good. If we have a posture of defending ourselves, we will
repel instead of draw sinners.

When we go to the beach, we know that there is a great
chance that the sun will offend our skin by burning us.
Therefore, we apply sunscreen. When we go fishing and
camping we expect mosquitoes to offend us by biting us, so
we apply insect repellant. We know that offenses are coming, so let's put on the full armor of God. Let's put on love
and forgive others before we leave our house or answer our
phones, amen! We know it is coming, so let's be wise as serpents and harmless as doves. We must remember that we are
not in a state of righteousness because of any works we have
done but because the grace of God has forgiven us. There is
nothing we could have possibly done that would earn our

salvation or forgiveness, so why do we want to make people do some kind of penitence before we forgive them? We are supposed to demonstrate manifestations of the will of God and how His grace will forgive.

When we have unforgiveness, we step out of the spirit and into the flesh. We can't be forgiven or healed and actually turn ourselves over to the tormentors. I believe we create most of our own warfare by responding improperly, contrary to the Word of God. We step out of unity and into division and have become guilty of the sin of hindering church growth.

We need to consider that when we get saved, we are baptized into the Body, and when we do things, they affect the whole Body; it's not just our business anymore.

# Chapter 3

# Horizontal Forgiveness

As a minister, a pastor, and a traveling evangelist, I see a lot of people in the Church proclaiming love to their God. There are even people out of Church who love God but hate the Church. Remember, the Church is people. There are many that hate the organized gathering of saints. Truly deception has crept into the Body of Christ. If we say that we love God, but hate our brothers or sisters, we remain in darkness. We lie.

*He that saith he is in the light, and hateth his brother, is in darkness even until now. He that loveth his brother abideth in the light, and there is none occasion of stumbling in him. But he that hateth his brother is in darkness, and walketh in darkness, and knoweth not whither he goeth, because that darkness hath blinded his eyes* (1 John 2:9-11).

The two most important commandments are as follows:

*Jesus said unto him, Thou shalt love the Lord thy God with all thy heart, and with all thy soul, and with all thy mind. This is the first and great commandment. And the second is like unto it, Thou shalt love thy neighbour as thyself* (Matthew 22:37-39).

The problem we run into here is everyone has a different definition of neighbor. In the Jewish culture, they were very segregated and didn't reach out to other cultures or races. If you weren't a Jew, you were called a dog or a heathen. It's a shame to say, but we still see that in some denominations today. They believe you aren't saved if you aren't from their church. God wants us to love one another as He has loved us, which is unconditionally.

God has shown me that many are willing to love and request forgiveness vertically, meaning from them to God and back. In the Jewish nation, they understood that once a year a priest went into the Holy of Holies and offered blood to cover the sins of Israel, and at certain times people could even offer sacrifices for individual sins. The priest did a corporate offering for the nation and then people would offer individual offerings at times for themselves.

Again, this was all vertical forgiveness from God to man. Humankind had the understanding at that time that only God could forgive. They even had a teaching that said love your neighbor and hate your enemy. However, Jesus came to change this. His message from Heaven was each individual person was responsible to forgive everyone and then seek forgiveness from God. The answer to earth's problems is found in forgiveness.

In the next few pages, I will show you in the Scriptures that, until Jesus, there wasn't any revelation to forgive horizontally, person to person.

*When Jesus saw their faith, He said unto the sick of the palsy, Son, thy sins be forgiven thee. But there was certain of the scribes sitting there, and reasoning in their hearts, Why doth this man thus speak blasphemies?* **who can forgive sins but God only?** (Mark 2:5-7)

Here we see Jesus forgiving a man's sins as an answer to his need for healing. The same power that forgives also heals, and when He forgives, His power is released. You will learn later that we are to be trained to network with Heaven and become distributors of forgiveness. Let's consider the Scripture on love and hate.

*Ye have heard that it hath been said, Thou shalt love thy neighbour, and hate thine enemy. But I say unto you, Love your enemies, bless them that curse you, do good to them that hate you, and pray for them which despitefully use you, and persecute you* (Matthew 5:43-44).

Because of this old tradition, they had a choice to love or hate. If your neighbor offended you, all you had to do was place him on your enemy list and now hate him. There was no accountability about walking in love, forgiveness, restoration, and so on. This was one of the reasons Jesus turned the religious world upside down. He came to destroy religion as it was known then. He came to remove the traditions of men. He came to teach love and forgiveness. The Jews were looking for a warrior Messiah who would conquer the Romans and restore Jerusalem to the Jews. They wanted a

Messiah king to set up a natural kingdom and do it just for them. They thought that through much bloodshed and loss of life, they could purchase a present-day, natural kingdom (which could always be lost if someone stronger came along).

Jesus came to set up an eternal, spiritual Kingdom which would cost Him His life and His blood, which was pure and clean. His Kingdom came through obedience even unto death. It came through submission, love, and forgiveness. Granted, later many saints would die for the Gospel's sake. All the apostles except John died a martyr's death. We see in Stephen's death in the Book of Acts that dying a martyr's death wasn't complete without forgiving and then requesting forgiveness from God on their behalf.

The power released by forgiving will assist us when we die and cross over and even assist us in resurrection. Let's look at Peter. He was a Jew and followed Jewish traditions and culture. He lived in Israel. I would say he would know what was taught there. He was ignorant about forgiving horizontally. He asked this question.

*Then came Peter to Him, and said, Lord, how oft shall my brother sin against me, and I forgive him? till seven times? Jesus saith unto him, I say not unto thee, Until seven times: but, Until seventy times seven* (Matthew 18:21-22).

Jesus began to teach that forgiving, which was only before seen as from God to man, now was from one person to another.

Earlier we read Mark 2:5-7, where Jesus healed a paralytic man lowered through a roof. When He stated, *"Thy sins be forgiven thee,"* everyone panicked because they knew that only God could forgive. As we become sons and daughters of God, we should be acting like God in the matter of loving unconditionally and forgiving. We saw earlier that Jesus taught that forgiveness shouldn't be an occasional action but a lifestyle—seventy times seven equals four hundred and ninety times a day. Isn't it amazing how we want to receive grace and forgiveness at that high a level if needed, but we don't want to give it?

Forgiveness is for those who do us wrong, not for those who do us right. Sometimes we act like forgiveness is rationed, like there is a shortage. Actually, when we were forgiven God gave us more than what we need. I believe that's why David said *"my cup runneth over"* (Ps. 23:5). We clearly see in the Scriptures that we are held accountable to give out whatever we have received from the Lord. *"Heal the sick, cleanse the lepers, raise the dead, cast out devils: freely ye have received, freely give"* (Matt. 10:8). This is more than a suggestion; this is a commission, a command. Earlier we saw that Jesus forgave and healed. They are intertwined; when we are forgiven—saved—it includes healing and deliverance.

In the Lord's Prayer, Jesus teaches us to pray. *"And forgive us our debts, as we forgive our debtors"* (Matt. 6:12). John the Baptist came with a message of repentance for the Kingdom of Heaven was at hand. Jesus said that if He cast out devils, it is at hand now (see Matt. 3:2; 12:28). The Scripture tells us John the Baptist came in the spirit of Elijah to restore the hearts of the children to the Father (see Luke 1:17). When the fullness of time came, the heavens opened to the shepherds and the angels communicated "peace on earth" and "good will toward men" (see Luke 2:14). I believe they were prophesying the coming of the Messiah. They knew the message He would bring forth on earth, which would ultimately bring peace. It wasn't a gospel of perfection, but a Gospel of forgiveness.

## Finding Peace

Since the Fall of Adam, there had been training and teaching of how we could approach God with offerings of blood to cover our sins. There were rules and regulations people had to follow actually over and above God's rule. Praise God I was born into the era of grace. Thank You, Jesus!

The only way there can be peace in the earth is when men and women and children learn to forgive and then receive forgiveness from God. Jesus was the last Lamb ever to be slain. The peace on earth the angels were talking about is a peace that the world knows not.

*Peace I leave with you, My peace I give unto you: not as the world giveth, give I unto you. Let not your heart be troubled, neither let it be afraid* (John 14:27).

Now His disciples have learned this new Kingdom isn't worried about what government is in place at the time, even if it is pagan or evil. The Kingdom of God will flourish regardless. They are now being taught to forgive not only their brothers, but their enemies also. In Christ's teaching we are taught to love and pray for the good of all humankind. Our natural minds sometimes go on tilt trying to understand God and His Kingdom principles, which must be spiritually discerned. We mustn't try to be in an organization like the Old Covenant where only one priest would go into God's presence then tell them what's up. We are all priests, so let us all go into His presence forgiving and being forgiven, having our minds opened to understand the Scripture and His ways. It now is beneficial for us to forgive.

> *For if ye forgive men their trespasses, your heavenly Father will also forgive you: but if ye forgive not men their trespasses, neither will your Father forgive your trespasses* (Matthew 6:14-15).

We must be prepared to forgive. Let us lower our expectations of people and let our stress level go down. Now let us raise our expectations of God and what He wants to do on this earth through us and others. One thing we all need to learn is that we need one another. The Scripture tells us that we don't fight against each other but against devils. We become the puppets of offense and the devil is the puppet master.

> *For we wrestle not against flesh and blood, but against principalities, against powers, against the rulers of the darkness of this world, against spiritual wickedness in high places* (Ephesians 6:12).

Continue reading in Ephesians and we see we are in a battle and we need to dress properly.

> *Wherefore take unto you the whole armour of God, that ye may be able to withstand in the evil day, and having done*

*all, to stand. Stand therefore, having your loins girt about with truth, and having on the breastplate of righteousness; and your feet shod with the preparation of the gospel of peace; above all, taking the shield of faith, wherewith ye shall be able to quench all the fiery darts of the wicked. And take the helmet of salvation, and the sword of the Spirit, which is the word of God: praying always with all prayer and supplication in the Spirit, and watching thereunto with all perseverance and supplication for all saints* (Ephesians 6:13-18).

When a brother or sister offends us, the devil is trying to steal friendships, cause us to break covenants, and steal the peace the Lord Jesus has left us here on this earth. The Kingdom of God is peace, righteousness, and joy in the Holy Ghost.

In order for us to get along, we must all take up our cross daily and crucify our flesh. I am convinced it will take us partnering with God to work with one another here on earth. We must start by becoming like little children to enter the Kingdom of God. The flesh hates everything of God. They disagree on everything.

*Because the carnal mind is enmity against God: for it is not subject to the law of God, neither indeed can be. So then they that are in the flesh cannot please God* (Romans 8:7-8).

So you ask, "What do we do?" We begin by humbling ourselves and submitting to God. *"Submit yourselves therefore to God. Resist the devil, and he will flee from you"* (James 4:7). We must take off the old man and place on the new man in Christ. This New Covenant not only teaches us to submit to God but to one another. Wives, submit to husbands, young ones submit to elders. We are to submit to overseers of our souls.

*Likewise, ye younger, submit yourselves unto the elder. Yea, all of you be subject one to another, and be clothed with humility: for God resisteth the proud, and giveth grace to the humble* (1 Peter 5:5).

But wait, there's more. Ephesians says, *"Submitting yourselves one to another in the fear of God"* (Eph. 5:21). Taking up the cross, crucifying our flesh daily, taking our thoughts captive and placing on our armor, pleading the blood, using the Name of Jesus, submitting first to God and then to one another—sounds like there might be a war going on. And indeed there is.

*Therefore rejoice, ye heavens, and ye that dwell in them. Woe to the inhabiters of the earth and of the sea! for the devil is come down unto you, having great wrath, because he knoweth that he hath but a short time* (Revelation 12:12).

*The thief cometh not, but for to steal, and to kill, and to destroy: I am come that they might have life, and that they might have it more abundantly* (John 10:10).

The devil subtracts by division. He constantly is causing strife, envy, bitterness, hatred, and murder. These are actually the works of the flesh, and he tries to keep us in the flesh and then amplify these traits of the fallen man. Why, you say? Because if he can keep us in the flesh, no one can please

God and we won't hear and obey and build the Kingdom or maintain peace, righteousness, and joy.

Remember, a house divided can't stand. God is love, and in order for us to love and walk together as a Body, we must forgive and work together as a Body. We must forgive and work tirelessly together to accomplish the Kingdom work. Our commission is so great. We need everyone working in the Spirit of love to accomplish this great task. That's why we need to learn of this horizontal forgiveness. Not only must we forgive people when they forgive us, we must be like Christ on the cross, interceding and requesting that God forgive them also. A selfish person can't accomplish this assignment from Heaven. He or she will spend all of their time consumed by self. This is a perfect reason we must die to ourselves and take up our cross and follow Jesus.

## Not About Me

I was getting ready to preach one service at a friend's church. As they were doing announcements, I was talking to God about a certain door to international television that had opened. In my mind, I asked why it was happening, because I knew I had done nothing to deserve it. As I walked up to the stage to take the microphone, the Lord spoke to me and said, "It's not about you."

I knew at that time it was the message He had given me and it was for the people who needed to hear it. I was a vessel, an instrument which had been chosen because of gifts in me. We are commanded by God to forgive and to love and preach this Gospel of forgiveness, heal the sick, and cast out devils.

*Faith moves God, but forgiveness releases His power.* Listen, it can no longer be about just you and God. We have to be right with people. We can't harbor unforgiveness, bitterness, and anger. It is sin. Let's get the hate out of our camp by forgiving and then loving again.

We learn from the Scripture and from our relationship with God through Christ that God is perfect, and He doesn't lie. We don't have to work at His side of the covenant with us. He says He'll never leave us nor forsake us (see Heb. 13:5). His thoughts toward us are good. We know that there is love and forgiveness flowing and available from Him. We can trust Him to hold up *His* end; we need to be working on *our* side of the covenant.

The devil knows how the Kingdom of Heaven works. He understands how spiritual principles work. He is a spirit and has been around for quite some time. His whole plan is to interfere with humankind and cause hate through offense, bitterness, and unforgiveness. He wants to kill as many people as he can before they get saved. He also wants to kill saved people so they never fulfill their destiny.

Remember, forgiveness releases God's power. Unforgiveness releases the devil's power. Forgiveness is the fruit of love. Unforgiveness is the fruit of hate. Satan knows that the Scripture states that love never fails. Therefore, if he causes division, strife, hate, and the like, then love has been nullified.

Why would He want to stop God's love through us?

Love never fails.

Love forgives.

Faith worketh by love.

If there is no love, then faith doesn't work, and we will receive nothing from the Lord. Without faith, it is impossible to please God. Many generals of past wars knew to cut off communication and then all incoming supplies. A Christian with no communication with Heaven and no incoming strength, power, or provision is usually a weak person. Now when we get offended, the first thing we want to do is withdraw from church and people. We are weaker by ourselves and easily defeated. The more people who withdraw from the Body, the weaker the Body becomes, that is, less resources, money, manpower, workers, volunteers, and so on.

Let's make a conscious decision to forgive, forget, and love one another. Let's do it for Christ's sake. If we will forgive, God's power and love are released and allowed to freely flow again. Heaven is perfect; however, earth and its inhabitants are a mess. God's plan is for us to love and forgive. The freer the flow of love, the more our faith will work, bringing Heaven to earth.

I believe that in this chapter I have shown you and hopefully convinced you for the need to reach out horizontally to one another and forgive, forget, and love. I'm talking about relationships from fathers to children, husbands to wives, brothers to sisters, cousins, neighbors and even strangers to strangers.

Forgive, forget, and love. *Faith moves God, but forgiveness releases His power.* Once His power has been released, slowly memories and feelings of the past will be healed.

It is definitely a high priority for God's children to get along and work together. If it's not high on our list of priorities, then we need to make some changes. Forgiveness is the power and one of our tools to bring God's Kingdom to earth. While we were still sinners, still wrong and living a sinful lifestyle set against Him, God forgave us for Christ's sake. You will find out in another chapter the different ways God has given us to help people get saved. Now we can use forgiveness to help convert people, bring them before God, and change their atmosphere so the Holy Spirit can begin to convict and then convert.

Begin to look around you. Are there relationships in your life that have been affected by offense, bitterness, rejection, and other like sins? Are there people who are not saved who need the saving grace of God's forgiveness? Hurry, tell them. Tell everyone before it is too late. Salvation and forgiveness are for right now—in this lifetime.

*Chapter 4*

# FORGIVING FROM THE CROSS

You and I know all too well that wherever you have people, you will have problems. It will always be. We can train people through teaching and preaching to cooperate with each other and become better team players, but offenses will still come. *"Then said He unto the disciples, It is impossible but that offenses will come: but woe unto him, through who they come!"* (Luke 17:1). Another Scripture tells us we will encounter trouble in the world.

> *These things I have spoken unto you, that in Me ye might have peace. In the world ye shall have tribulation: but be of good cheer; I have overcome the world* (John 16:33).

We have now plainly been told by our Savior and King, Jesus Christ, that everything isn't always going to go just right. Don't be shocked, but there are those out there who don't play well with others. Now the Lord hasn't left us here in a world of trials, tribulation, and troubles without wisdom available to us on how to cope and even be victorious. All through this book you will read experiences where people have been hurt, backstabbed, abandoned. No matter what wrong has happened to you, your best and only godly response is to forgive.

I will repeat a statement I heard a minister make, "Harboring unforgiveness is like you drinking poison and expecting the other person to die." It will first hurt you and then others around you. It will cause you to turn on those you love who haven't done you wrong.

*Follow peace with all men, and holiness, without which no man shall see the Lord: looking diligently lest any man fail of the grace of God; lest any root of bitterness springing up trouble you, and thereby many be defiled* (Hebrews 12:14-15).

There is a saying: "Hurt people hurt people." This is so true. Abused people abuse people. Abandoned people abandon people. Molested people molest people, and so on. But praise God, healed people heal people. In Hebrews 12:15 it says, *"lest any root of bitterness* [springs] *up."* In order for a root of bitterness to spring up there must be a seed planted and then protected so it could begin the growing process.

The seed for bitterness is a seed of offense turned to unforgiveness. In order for it to begin to grow, we must meditate, ponder, and rehearse the offense.

We cannot allow wrongdoing and offense to begin to build strongholds of unforgiveness in our hearts. This includes all offenses:

- Murder
- Rape, including date rape

- Beatings
- Domestic violence
- Child abuse
- Theft, robbery
- Lying, false accusations
- Church splits, divisions

No matter how bad the crime or how wronged we have been, we must forgive. This doesn't excuse someone's behavior or make what they did right. It simply positions you to begin your healing process. The whole point of this chapter is to teach you to prevent the wrong seed from being planted in your heart.

Let's look at Christ's example at Calvary. Here we see the creation attempting to murder the Creator. It actually was the Creator laying down His life to make salvation available for the creation. Neither the people nor the principalities truly knew who they were dealing with. If Israel would have had their eyes opened to know Him like Peter had, they wouldn't have crucified Him.

Peter's revelation came from fellowship with Him, being in His presence, watching how He dealt with other humans in a superhuman way. Jesus dealt with people different from all other religious leaders, and so should we as His disciples. Jesus was the first human Temple of God, and when the rivers of life flowed out of Jesus, revelation from the Father in Heaven opened Peter's eyes to the truth.

Unforgiveness blocks and dams up the river of life and revelation from Heaven. It hinders His Kingdom from coming to earth. It hinders all prayers from being answered. Unforgiveness stops all deliveries from Heaven. Prayers answered are grace being released. When grace is not released, all that is left is judgment and torment. We need grace to survive in this fallen world.

This next Scripture shows my point of their acting in ignorance. First Corinthians 2:8 says, *"Which none of the princes of this world knew: for had they known it, they would not have crucified the Lord of glory."* Jesus had already been mocked, falsely accused, ridiculed, betrayed, abandoned by God, beaten badly, had thorns pressed upon His head, punched, His beard pulled out, and placed on the cross.

- The pain of the thorns
- The pain of the nails in His hands and feet
- The pain of His body weight on His hands and feet
- The pain of being pierced in His side
- The intense heat, hunger, and thirst
- People chanting, "crucify Him" and "let Him save Himself, He saved others"

In all that happened on the cross, we are given a key. Right while this is going on, even after He became sin and experienced separation from God, Christ forgave them and spoke in their defense by saying, *"Father, forgive them, for they know not what they do..."* (Luke 23:34).

We see here that the key to keeping seeds of offense from getting in our heart, turning it hard, then spreading roots of bitterness, is to forgive right while the offense is happening. Right from the cross He spoke. Having a shield of forgiveness neutralizes the seed of offense. It can't grow in soil treated with the power of God released when forgiveness is in operation.

He even took it to a higher level and then spoke in their defense and interceded on their behalf.

> *And when they were come to the place, which is called Calvary, there they crucified Him, and the malefactors, one on the right hand, and the other on the left. Then said Jesus, Father, forgive them; for they know not what they do. And they parted His raiment, and cast lots. And the people stood beholding. And the rulers also with them derided Him, saying, He saved others; let Him save Himself, if He be Christ, the chosen of God. And the soldiers also mocked Him, coming to Him, and offering Him vinegar, and saying, If Thou be the king of the Jews, save Thyself* (Luke 23:33-37).

I have found that when we forgive people who offend us while it is happening and then intercede for them, our recovery time from the offense is instant. Jesus wouldn't have said, *"it is finished,"* without forgiving and praying.

We see in God's Word that after the resurrection, He ascended to Heaven at the right hand of the Father where He prays (intercedes) daily. He already proved His worth to be an intercessor by interceding for those who were being used to kill Him.

## Know Your Identity

I guess the reason Jesus was able to forgive immediately was that He knew who He was, where He was from, and where He was going. He didn't have an identity problem.

By being in prayer often and always keeping in communion with the Holy Spirit and the Father, he was able to keep His cool, so to speak.

The Scripture tells us He went often to pray. I think this is a key. You see, by praying often, we are crucifying the flesh and working self-control over the soul. It is in the area of the soul, or the emotions, where offense begins. We read that sin was first conceived in the heart of satan. Imaginations will grow offense and hatred if fed by the soul.

The imagination surrendered to the Spirit will give faith a place to grow, and then we should meditate on the Word of God. Jesus was kept humble by always being in the presence of Almighty God. It is pride in our fallen nature that gets offended. We say, "How dare someone do this to me?" Now there are cases where we get hurt, abuses or crimes which have nothing to do with pride, but many of the minor offenses are when we feel we have been disrespected. Because Jesus always listened to the Father, He knew what to say and how to respond. Actually, the Holy Spirit would tell Him of things to come. He could prayerfully prepare Himself through the Word. Through building Himself in prayer, He received wisdom on how to deal with situations. I'm convinced if we spend more time in prayer receiving from our Father, we will attain greater maturity.

*And it came to pass in those days, that He went out into a mountain to pray, and continued all night in prayer to God* (Luke 6:12).

We become deceived and fall right into the plan of the devil by getting angry at the people who say and do things that hurt us. Remember, we are told we don't fight against people, but against spirits who manipulate people. If we really pay attention to this, then if we get angry, we need to get angry at the devil and forgive and pray for the person being used to hurt or causing problems.

*For we wrestle not against flesh and blood, but against principalities, against powers, against the rulers of the darkness of this world, against spiritual wickedness in high places* (Ephesians 6:12).

Let's jump ahead to verse 18:

*Praying always with all prayer and supplication in the Spirit, and watching thereunto with all perseverance and supplication for all saints* (Ephesians 6:18).

When you read the whole passage from 12 through 18, you will see it tells us we don't fight against people, but devils. Now you can dress for spiritual battles knowing where all this warfare originates. The people caught up in it are deceived and have been taken captive at the devil's will. Let's pray for them. First, forgive them, releasing God's power which repels the warfare, and then pray they would become free and productive in God's Kingdom.

I'm convinced that if you're easily offended, you are not as mature as you think you are and are still ignorant in spiritual things. Now wait a minute before you get offended at me while you are reading a book on forgiveness. Finish it first, and you will see I am trying to give you the truth right up front. This is truth that I've learned through revelation and practical application.

Like Jesus we must forgive from the cross, right while it is happening. The quicker you release and forgive, the quicker God's power is released to fix and prevent problems. I've said in other chapters that knowing that offenses are going to happen, we must dress properly in our armor and pray up. We must train ourselves to respond properly by forgiving, loving, and responding immediately. Do this, and you have protected your soul from seeds of offense, and you can begin intercession for the captive souls that cause strife, division, and scattering of the sheep. Through spending time in the Word of God, and time with the God of the Word, dressing always in the armor, and allowing God's love to flow through us, we can release forgiveness. Jesus was able to grant forgiveness and pray for forgiveness. When the woman was caught in adultery, He didn't make her wait for days.

*And the scribes and Pharisees brought unto Him a woman taken in adultery; and when they had set her in the midst, they say unto Him, Master, this woman was taken in adultery, in the very act. Now Moses in the law commanded us, that such should be stoned: but what sayest Thou? This they said, tempting Him, that they might have to accuse Him. But Jesus stooped down, and with His finger wrote on the ground, as though He heard them not. So when they continued asking Him, He lifted up Himself, and said unto them, He that is without sin among you, let him first cast a stone at her. And again He stooped down, and wrote on the ground. And they which heard it, being convicted by their own conscience, went out one by one, beginning at the eldest, even unto*

*the last: and Jesus was left alone, and the woman stand-*
*ing in the midst. When Jesus had lifted up Himself, and*
*saw none but the woman, He said unto her, Woman,*
*where are those thine accusers? hath no man condemned*
*thee? She said, No man, Lord. And Jesus said unto her,*
*Neither do I condemn thee: go, and sin no more* (John
8:3-11).

When I first heard this story, I was amazed at how
quickly Jesus removed the condemnation and gave
forgiveness. He knows you have to deal with seeds of condemnation, offense, and bitterness. Words have power. We
mustn't allow them to have any soil to be planted in to
begin to grow.

*Death and life are in the power of the tongue: and they*
*that love it shall eat the fruit thereof* (Proverbs 18:21).

We see that Jesus was willing to allow the man on the
cross to be one of the first to benefit from the work of the
cross. He forgave the woman caught in adultery and the
man let down through the roof. His examples show us that
we are to quickly forgive, remit sins, and share the love we
have received from the Father. It is such an important key to
forgive and try to be forgiven as soon as possible. Again, so
seeds of offense do not start to grow in us or in others. Seeds
of offense grow roots of bitterness which bring a harvest
of torment, sickness, and disease, even phobia, fears, anger,
and outburst of rage.

*Looking diligently lest any man fail of the grace of God;*
*lest any root of bitterness springing up trouble you, and*
*thereby many be defiled* (Hebrews 12:15).

# Taking Responsibility

I pray the Holy Spirit convicts you as you read this and unveils any blind spots or old offenses. You can then through Him repent, confess, forgive, and release yourselves, others, and even God.

1. Repentance activates the need for acceptance of Christ's salvation and forgiveness.
2. Acceptance begins the process of forgiveness.
3. Forgiveness empowers one to stop sinning.
4. Knowing one has been forgiven activates and releases a love we have never known, experienced, or walked in.

In Luke we see Jesus giving forgiveness:

*Wherefore I say unto thee, Her sins, which are many, are forgiven; for she loved much: but to whom little is forgiven, the same loveth little* (Luke 7:47).

God's love caused Him to give and send His Son. God's love causes Him to always forgive when we repent. If we will allow the love of God to be shed abroad in our hearts, we too will be empowered to give freely, forgive always, and love unconditionally.

I always wondered why Jesus told the woman caught in adultery to go and sin no more. I thought the reason she was caught was because she didn't have control or the power not to do this. Then I realized that in the words "go and sin no more" was the power to accomplish what she had been told to do. This word to her was prophetic. He saw her as she was about to become. We must remember that the Gospel, the words of Jesus, is the power of salvation. Whatever situation I'm in, I seek Christ for a "now word." Once I receive that "now word," I understand that in that word is the power to accomplish the task. He forgave her and His power was released in His word for her to sin no more.

I have said before, but will repeat it again. *Faith moves God, but forgiveness releases His power.*

- Forgiveness repels sin.
- Forgiveness repels rejections.
- Forgiveness repels sickness.
- Forgiveness repels demons.
- Forgiveness repels hell.

We must first take responsibility for our lives and wrongdoings. Then we can receive forgiveness. If we educate ourselves in the Word, then we will come to our understanding that we need to start each day in the presence of the Lord worshiping, praising, and bringing our supplication before the Lord. We mustn't forget to cast our cares upon the Lord. We weren't created to carry stress, anxiety, and fear. If this has been warfare in your life, then once you get free, start your day in His presence worshiping. Give to God the things you weren't created to handle, and then receive from Him a daily infilling of peace, righteousness, and joy. Request Him to fill all the voids in your soul with love and forgiveness. You will come out of the presence of the Lord healed, forgiven, sealed by the blood, and filled with His love. Now you will be better equipped to handle daily matters dealing with one another. We are dressed in the armor, listening to the Holy Spirit, and ready to distribute Heaven's answer to earth's problems by forgiving and releasing His power.

We've now received from the Lord. We're dressed properly. We understand who the enemy is, so let's instantly forgive those who hurt us. Every offense, as it comes, return evil with good. Forgive, forget, and love. Now you become like Teflon, and offense doesn't stick to you. You don't have to spend days, weeks, months, and even years trying to get free from hurts, offenses, and wrongdoings.

There are so many people whose today and tomorrow has ceased—placed on hold and literally tormented by what someone did or didn't do to them in their yesterday. Each new day is another chance to be done wrong and offended. It's going to happen, so make a decision not to get angry or offended and *immediately* forgive. These offenses and wrong-doings that come against us could be called storms. Let's see what the Bible has to say about us and storms in Matthew:

*Therefore whosoever heareth these sayings of Mine, and doeth them, I will liken him unto a wise man, which built his house upon a rock: and the rain descended, and the floods came, and the winds blew, and beat upon that house; and it fell not: for it was founded upon a rock. And every one that heareth these sayings of Mine, and doeth them not, shall be likened unto a foolish man, which built his house upon the sand: and the rain descended, and the floods came, and the winds blew, and beat upon that house; and it fell: and great was the fall of it* (Matthew 7:24-27).

When we obey the Word, love, and forgive, we will come through the storms and attacks strong and with a mature faith. If we don't, fear, torment, and destruction lie in wait for us. Praise God that He has shared with us in His Word how to be successful in His Kingdom. I always want to be forgiven and loved, so I want to sow it. Begin loving and forgiving now from the cross.

I want you to remember when Jesus was forgiving while on the cross, He didn't do it after they repented or changed their ways. Actually, the only one who repented was the former thief on the cross beside Him. The people, scribes, and Pharisees were still mocking Him. The Roman soldiers were gambling and casting lots for His robe. No one was taking Him down and letting Him live. They were still in the process of sinning against Him. You can't be guaranteed that your forgiveness will change others, but you will be changed, set free, and remain free.

We see that Jesus and others, before they died, dealt with forgiving and praying for their accusers, asking God to forgive them. No matter what sin has transgressed against you, no matter how bad, quickly forgive and release before your harvest of torment comes. God so loved, He gave. God so loved, He forgave, and He will answer the cry of any soul who calls on the name of the Lord.

In our personal lives, we will learn to walk in the power of forgiveness, thereby walking in the power of God. It will repel sickness and disease, along with any torment that is attacking you and your family's lives.

In our church walk, we need to network with Heaven and distribute the power of forgiveness. We do that by loving, leading by example, forgiving the minute something happens so we can stay in the Spirit and not in the flesh. Many people need someone to teach them how to forgive from the cross, how to recover from the torment, assignments, and strategies the enemy has used against us.

It's a greater Gospel call to walk in love and forgiveness. Think of all the lost people who don't really know they can be forgiven. Many have only heard the gospel of perfection, but you can take them the Gospel of forgiveness. Souls in darkness need to see your light. They have been strangled and consumed by demons, and now possess no strength from which to fight. Please unselfishly teach the lost there is power to be obtained when we forgive.

Let me make something clear about what I mean when I say forgiving from the cross. The cross is the only reason that we can be forgiven. The Scripture tells us without the shedding of blood there is no remission of sins (see Heb. 9:22). It also tells us the life is in the blood (see Lev. 17:11). Jesus let His life in His blood be poured out on the earth still stained with Abel's blood which was crying for vengeance. And that moment, vengeance was had by the Lord. But His vengeance was so different from yours or mine. We would have made people pay. Instead, Jesus became flesh to die, and with His perfect, sinless blood redeemed both humankind and our deeds. When we become forgiven we are removed from paying for the penalty of sin, and we become born again only because of the cross and its statement of forgiveness.

Words have power. Powerful, godly words become answered prayer. His example to all of us is to forgive while we are being wronged.

When God planned to correct earth's problems, He planned that Christ would die and shed His blood to redeem us. It even says that Christ hung on a tree to become a curse so that the blessings of Abraham could come on the Gentiles. While we are alive, let's unselfishly forgive, forget, and love. Tell people everywhere that forgiveness is available vertically and horizontally because of Christ and the cross.

*Chapter 5*

# FORGIVENESS IS A KEY

Remember, in Chapter 1 humankind surrendered to temptation and all the natural creation and spiritual humankind was affected. The Heavenly Father had decided that the key to unlock this catastrophe would be a perfect sacrifice and then forgiveness. Before the foundation of the world, forgiveness was set as part of the redemption package. Now don't be mistaken—there is no forgiveness or remission of sin apart from the blood of Jesus. Salvation is, and always will be, a gift from the grace of God. But this gift that has been given is that He has forgiven us.

*For by grace are ye saved through faith; and that not of yourselves: it is the gift of God: not of works, lest any man should boast* (Ephesians 2:8-9).

Let's remember that *faith moves God, but forgiveness releases His power.* There is power in forgiveness. There is power in the blood. There is power in His Word. There is truly power in His Name. I am about to preach myself into answering my own altar call. I'm about to shout, "Glory to God!"

If you are having a bad day and nothing is going right, stop and ask yourself, "Am I saved?" If your answer is yes, then rejoice and shout, "I'm not going to hell!" It should change your whole perspective on life. We must not forget what the Lord has done for us, where we were and where we were headed and how we have been delivered. We have received forgiveness. It is like a seed that has been placed in our hearts. We are to be good stewards of the forgiveness He has given us. You received it, now give it. Don't let me hear you say that you don't have any forgiveness to give. Talking about forgiveness, Matthew says:

> *And as ye go, preach, saying, The kingdom of heaven is at hand. Heal the sick, cleanse the lepers, raise the dead, cast out devils: freely ye have received, freely give* (Matthew 10:7-8).

The Old Covenant taught, "Love your neighbors and hate your enemies." Jesus brought a new teaching about loving everyone regardless of race, religion, financial status, et cetera.

> *But I say unto you, Love your enemies, bless them that curse you, do good to them that hate you, and pray for them which despitefully use you, and persecute you; that ye may be the children of your Father which is in heaven: for He maketh His sun to rise on the evil and on the good, and sendeth rain on the just and on the unjust.... Be ye therefore perfect, even as your Father which is in heaven is perfect* (Matthew 5:44-45,48).

In context, "be perfect" means simply love and forgive and do good for everyone. Be perfect in forgiving and loving.

In verse 44, you see that if you accomplish this, then the door is open for you to be openly called one of the children of your Father in Heaven. Forgiveness protects in so many ways:

- From sickness and disease
- From torment and insanity and phobias
- It repels hell, the second death.

I will never forget 26 years ago when the Lord forgave me, and the bondage of sin and death which had held me captive for so long was unlocked by the key of His forgiveness which released His power. Fear, alcoholism, and addictions to cigarettes, sex, and drugs were unchained from me and those doors closed. Praise God! Praise God!

Since then I have seen thousands get free from sin, depression and insanity, addictions, and bondages of all types.

*And I will give unto thee the keys of the kingdom of heaven: and whatsoever thou shalt bind on earth shall be bound in heaven: and whatsoever thou shalt loose on earth shall be loosed in heaven* (Matthew 16:19).

When Jesus told Peter He was giving him the keys to the Kingdom, we can see Jesus telling His disciples that one of the keys to the Kingdom of Heaven was the revelation that He was the Christ.

Another key is found in John 20:23: *"Whose soever sins ye remit, they are remitted unto them; and whose soever sins ye retain, they are retained."* Believing in the revelation of the perfect sacrifice and the One who could forgive and then receiving power to forgive people are truly keys that open Heaven for us and close hell. Forgiveness begins the release of the supernatural power from Heaven on our behalf when we call on His Name. This power is revealed in many ways, however He chooses. It may come as salvation from our sins. It may come as healing to our wounded emotions or broken body. It may bring peace to a tormented mind. Nevertheless, His power is released from Heaven when He or we make a decision to forgive. A true manifestation of the character of God is released through us when we give and when we forgive. This isn't the nature of the fallen man. We want to get even, get revenge. We want to disrespect those who have disrespected us.

Human love is conditional. Do what we want, and then we will love you and fellowship with you. God's love is supernatural; His love is unconditional. He loves regardless. There are conditions and principles in this Kingdom, but His love is unconditional. *"But God commendeth His love toward us, in that, while we were yet sinners, Christ died for us."* (Rom. 5:8). He loved us and was willing to forgive us while we were still in the wrong. Reading this, hearing this is one thing. But to actually begin to walk in this truly is taking up His cross and following Him. That's right, this means daily sacrifice and taking your thoughts captive depending on how strong the habit of unforgiveness has grown. How long and how far has it gotten out of control in your life? Only you and God know the answer to this. His will is to see you free from this bondage. Ask His help, repent to Him, and watch His power begin to be released in your life.

To love and forgive is a manifestation of Christ's Spirit. To hate and hold unforgiveness is a manifestation of an antichrist spirit. There is a Spirit of truth and a spirit of the world which will run your life. Choose this day whom you will serve. We can't just receive forgiveness of sins. We need to receive Christ's teaching and doctrine.

# A Heart Issue

As I have prayed with many people over the years and shared this message, I've constantly run into people who tell me they have already forgiven the people who have hurt them. They say they have let it go, but they still are haunted by the past, and when they see the people or hear of the churches that have hurt them, they feel the same sickening feeling. They still have sickness, pain, and torment.

Let's take a moment and realize that we can say things with our lips that do not reach down into our hearts. You can line a thousand people up and have them pray the sinner's prayer, but if there is no conviction in their hearts, if there is no godly sorrow, then none of them will get saved. So many people have manipulated people into going to church, praying prayers, and even giving. None of these religious works will accomplish anything unless the Holy Spirit is the one doing the work in the hearts of men and women. If the Holy Spirit has convicted our hearts when we hear the teaching on salvation and forgiveness, then it will be a heart cry instead of an echo from our lips.

Some people will only repeat words to get a preacher off their backs.

I want to show you some Scriptures that will prove exactly what I am saying. When the Holy Spirit breathes on the Word of God, it becomes alive and convicts. Our proper response is to repent. *"For godly sorrow worketh repentance to salvation not to be repented of: but the sorrow of the world worketh death"* (2 Cor. 7:10). Truly we need to yield our souls and our emotions to the Holy Spirit. How do we do that? I am so glad you asked. Other people might explain it differently, but I just stick with "believe in my heart and confess, pray, or decree the Word."

So in this situation I pray, "Holy Spirit, I choose of my own free will to yield to You. I surrender my soul and emotions to You. Do whatever needs to be done. Search and reveal to me whatever I need to do or to pray, repent of, if I need to fast, etc. Please help me to become whole. Help me to be able to leave the torment of my past and let it go, so that I can fulfill my call and destiny."

Spend a week or so seriously praying this way and listen for the voice of the Holy Spirit. Now He may reveal it some other way than just talking to you. It may come while reading the Word as a Scripture just jumps out at you. Certain memories may come back to you. A relative or friend may remind you of something that hurt you.

*And his lord was wroth, and delivered him to the tormentors, till he should pay all that was due unto him. So likewise shall My heavenly Father do also unto you, if ye from your hearts forgive not every one his brother their trespasses* (Matthew 18:34-35).

It goes back to forgiving from our hearts. The problem is, when you and I get hurt, sometimes we tend to block out or hide in our souls these memories and oh, how the years go by so quickly. This is why we need to trust God to show us old and hidden pains and offenses so we can deal with them once and for all. Let's through Christ defeat the devil in our lives and get free.

Now some hurts, offenses, and bitterness are quite evident and we don't need anyone reminding us because we rehearse them daily. Did you know that when you rehearse these things, you have actually been watering them and building a mental stronghold of torment? I have spent hours and days in my office and on the phone with people from all around the world who have spent years tormented, their lives on hold, accomplishing absolutely nothing because of what they had done or what someone had done to them. Rehearsing these offenses had built strongholds that would for a lifetime keep them in bondage unless someone like me who had this message would come along and teach and pray and set them free in the name of the Lord. Because I know that so many people have forgiven with their lips and not their hearts, I come up with what I call "the conscious decision" prayer.

This means that I deliberately override my subconscious, where I have hidden hurts and pains, and from my heart I choose to forgive everyone who has hurt me or done me wrong. I forgive myself, and I forgive God if I'm angry at

Him. I release all the past and I let it go. No one has to repay me, perform for me, or do any type of works. I freely forgive.

Let's break it down into three parts.

1. People who have hurt us
2. Things we have done wrong
3. Being mad at God

## Unforgiveness Toward Others

In our society we have created what we call right behavior and wrong behavior. When people do what we consider wrong behavior, we become offended. When people don't do what we feel we deserve, we also become offended. So we get hurt by what people do or by what they don't do. If a father doesn't say "I love you," if he wasn't there, if he didn't provide for us, we feel rejected and suffer abandonment, which will grow a root of bitterness. Some offenses are minor. People said something, criticized us, or started gossip. These hurt our feelings also, but are easier to recover from if we work on it.

Now, there are other offenses, such as if someone verbally and mentally abused you or physically or sexually abused you or murdered a loved one. When we look at the different sins of offense, there appear to be different levels. But seriously, sin is sin.

Let me make something perfectly clear. As I am teaching people to forgive, this does not mean that the offender is innocent. Forgiving it doesn't mean it is OK. It's you taking a step of faith to be like God. Remember, God your Father gives and forgives. We are His children, so we need to give and forgive also. When you forgive, it is an act that must be done in the Spirit of God's supernatural love. We must forgive and release what happens in the natural.

Abuse—mental, physical, and sexual—almost always takes longer to heal from, and that's OK. Remember, your soul and body and mind have been violated. It is for your benefit that I am encouraging you to make a conscious decision to forgive and release. It actually begins your healing. It removes the tormentor's legal right to be there. After you forgive, you are going to have to daily rehearse, "I have made a decision to forgive. I have decided to release."

I highly recommend finding numerous Scriptures on forgiveness and love, Scriptures against fear, and on having a sound mind. A reliable Christian support group is also important. Humble yourself and see your pastor. Have counseling sessions to reinforce the fact that you are important and that there is a place in the Body for you. Everyone heals at a different speed. Don't be hard on yourself. Remember, God loves you and so do we. Before the Lord brought forgiveness into the picture, we were imprisoned in a fallen body, headed to hell for eternity. Our spirit, which is eternal, must exist somewhere for all eternity. There are two choices—one with God in eternal life, or in an eternal prison, the lake of fire.

So when the Lord offered forgiveness, it was and is a key that can unlock our eternal destiny and unlock us from the tormenting prison that comes from unforgiveness. Remember the very phrase that started this book to begin with—*Faith moves God, but forgiveness releases His power.*

Let's think about something. If forgiveness releases God's power, then unforgiveness releases the devil's power over us. Now, no matter what has been done to us or not done for us, the proper and godly response is to forgive. Let's choose to forgive, forget, and love with God's love. We will talk about forgetting toward the end of this chapter. That's a whole other issue.

## Unforgiveness Toward Self

I remember praying with a lady who kept saying, "I have forgiven everyone, even God, for anything and everything, and I am still miserable and sick. I can't get healed." I listened for a while and let her vent. I asked her to humor me and pray the conscious decision prayer with me. She agreed, and when we got to the part where I had her say, "I forgive myself for any failure," she started sobbing. She was so angry at herself because she kept making the same mistakes over and over again. She had such a high standard for herself in her own mind. Really, she held everyone to those same high standards. I taught her that if she would lower her expectations of people, her stress level would go down. She agreed. Then I showed her that she was too hard on herself. She had actually been raised by very critical parents. She recognized this fault, repented, and forgave herself. Instantly God's power was released. It overpowered satan's power, and she was instantly healed.

Time and time again, I have seen people who were too hard on themselves or wouldn't forgive themselves for sins that hurt others. Maybe they were in an accident driving a vehicle and the other party was killed. Maybe they blame themselves over a divorce or loss of a family member. The list can go on and on. But it is still the will of God that we forgive others and ourselves. We need to take a minute to understand that having unforgiveness toward others, ourselves, or even God is sin. The only way we can walk in bitterness, unforgiveness, and hate is to be in the flesh. Anything that is not faith is sin. Once we choose to forgive and see it is wrong and not the will of God, we need to repent and ask God to forgive us.

*If we confess our sins, He is faithful and just to forgive us our sins, and to cleanse us from all unrighteousness* (1 John 1:9).

We need to decide from the moment we wake up each day to choose to walk in the Spirit of God, being a doer of the Word of God, so we won't be in the flesh and be found not pleasing to God.

*He that saith, I know Him, and keepeth not His commandments, is a liar, and the truth is not in him. But whoso keepeth His word, in him verily is the love of God perfected: hereby know we that we are in Him* (1 John 2:4-5).

We see a wonderful truth here that in him who keeps His Word, the love of God is perfected. Look at this Scripture.

*There is no fear in love; but perfect love casteth out fear: because fear hath torment. He that feareth is not made perfect in love* (1 John 4:18).

Once we become doers of the Word and every day take up our cross, resist satan, and submit to God, we are seeing that things are becoming quieter in our minds. By keeping the Word, love is perfected, and as it is perfected, fear is driven from our lives.

Can you see why we need to love and forgive ourselves for past mistakes and sins? It is so we can be perfected, yielding ourselves to be used by God. Remember, the enemy will always try to get you to think on things of your past and tell you that you are not really saved, that God hasn't forgiven you. He is always telling you you're a failure and will never amount to anything. Tell him to shut up and be gone, because he is a liar and we ought not have fellowship with darkness. Don't hang out and talk with the devil. Hang out and talk with the Holy Ghost. He can give you love, wisdom, and comfort. He will show you things to come. He works in us and convicts us. The devil lies to us and condemns us.

Let's look again at First John.

*He that saith he is in the light, and hateth his brother, is in darkness even until now. He that loveth his brother abideth in the light, and there is none occasion of stumbling in him* (1 John 2:9-10).

I believe this describes you loving others and even yourself. If we are to love others as we love ourselves, and we don't love ourselves, we won't be very successful. Hurt people hurt people. Healed people heal people. Forgiven people love, so when we are given the gift of forgiveness, we are releasing God's power and His love.

*Let no corrupt communication proceed out of your mouth, but that which is good to the use of edifying, that it may minister grace unto the hearers. And grieve not the Holy Spirit of God, whereby ye are sealed unto the day of redemption. Let all bitterness, and wrath, and anger, and clamour, and evil speaking, be put away from you, with all malice: and be ye kind one to another, tenderhearted, forgiving one another, even as God for Christ's sake hath forgiven you* (Ephesians 4:29-32).

## Unforgiveness Toward God

This is actually more common and widespread than you'd ever imagine. The devil subtracts by division. He is always telling people, "If God is a good God, then why did He allow this to happen or that to happen?" As a pastor, I've had to do funerals for young people who have died in car accidents as a result of drinking and driving. Some of the relatives were angry at God for killing their boy and taking him before his time. Let me stand up and say, God shouldn't be blamed when a person mixes alcohol and driving. It's not God. It was the person's choice.

I have a simple two-part theology that I feel explains everything. Here it is:

1. God is good.

2. The devil is bad.

*The thief cometh not, but for to steal, and to kill, and to destroy: I am come that they might have life, and that they might have it more abundantly* (John 10:10).

Even when storms, earthquakes, or hurricanes happen, people call it an act of God. He gets blamed for anything that goes wrong, while anything going right we take credit for. Often, God gets blamed when people pray out of the will of God and ask for things to fulfill their lust or pray for things that will hurt them. Maybe the person isn't old enough or mature enough spiritually. When they don't get their prayers answered, they get angry at God. The person might have doubt or be a double-minded individual; therefore, it is their fault prayers were not answered. Yet God gets blamed. Hear the Word when it says:

*But let him ask in faith, nothing wavering. For he that wavereth is like a wave of the sea driven with the wind and tossed. For let not that man think that he shall receive any thing of the Lord. A double minded man is unstable in all his ways* (James 1:6-8).

Starting in Genesis with the very first man, God got blamed. Adam told God the problem was "the woman You gave me" (see Gen. 3:12). That's right—when things go wrong, it's so easy to blame God for premature deaths, storms, and tragedies. People need to begin to take responsibility for their own actions. The reason they don't is because if they do, they are responsible to correct wrongs and make things right. Even if you have Scripture to stand on and present your case before God, and you've removed all doubt and unbelief from your heart, if your prayer request involves another person, God will not go against their will. He's not a control freak like we can become. He wants people to love Him and serve Him because they choose to.

Let's say there is a wonderful Christian woman who attends church, pays her tithes, gives to the poor, volunteers her time, and is faithful. Her heart is right before the Lord. Doesn't that seem like a pretty perfect picture? Now let's say that her husband is not saved or has backslidden and finds another woman and leaves her. The woman believes, prays, and fasts, and does all she knows to do, but the husband doesn't repent or come home. It appears God didn't help her or answer her prayer. God is bound by His Word to allow all people to have a free will. If He goes against their will, He now acts like satan.

I have seen many women and men angry at God because He didn't fix the problems in their lives. I believe God would love to fix all these problems, but again, there are laws of the universe, and what people sow they will reap. He won't go against another's will.

If you have anything in your heart held against God where you have judged God harshly, forgive, and then ask Him to forgive you. He is a loving Father, and He understands you have been hurt and blinded by the fight or trial that you've been through.

As a pastor, I've known good Christians who died of disease before their time, and I knew that the person wanted to be healed. They believed in healing, all their family was in agreement, and it appeared that God wasn't hearing them and they died. Or perhaps your issue is a divorce, a death, a bankruptcy, children, or employment; I encourage you that God isn't the one at fault. I may not have all the answers, but one thing I do know: God is love and He wants to comfort you through your loss or trial. Make a conscious decision to forgive God and no longer hold Him responsible.

Wow, it seems we are finding out that offense, bitterness, and unforgiveness is used as a larger tool of the devil than we have ever known. Let's make a decision to be educated by God to forgive and to love. Let's separate what was done from the person like God has done for us. *"As far as the east is from the west, so far hath He removed our transgressions from us"* (Ps. 103:12).

Just as God not only forgives, but separates the deed from us, when thoughts of an offense come, we need to say out loud, "No, devil, shut up. I have forgiven that person, myself, or God, and I have released them from any penalty." Sometimes it takes many times of taking our thoughts captive. We rehearse the offense for years, but let's change and rehearse that we have forgiven and released. Repetition is the mother of breakthrough. Tear down demonic strongholds and build godly strongholds with the Word of God. *Faith moves God, but forgiveness releases His power.*

*Chapter 6*

# Healing and Deliverance

I constantly felt led and drawn to sick and lame people. I wanted to see them set free, healed, and delivered. Every opportunity to pray for the sick, I jumped on. I used to go to stores and look for people limping and wearing hearing aids, walking with canes, etc. I would try to find any excuse to pray for people, witness to them, and tell them what great things the Lord had done for me. I had been bound for years by drugs and alcohol. Demons had oppressed and tormented my mind with fear—fear of rejection and failure.

My encounter on that hill that day when I called on His Name forever changed me, my destiny, and since then, the lives of many. I've had an experience and know I've got something to say. I no longer believe Jesus is Lord, I know that I know. My "knower" was activated. Saved, delivered, transformed, and born again. I am now a new creature in Christ Jesus, all things of old are passed away. I get excited just writing about the experience.

Having been to Africa and on the mission field in other countries, I had seen other ministers perform great miracles and healings in Jesus' Name. When I prayed, occasionally people would be healed, but not like the results others were seeing. I began to cry out to God to increase the power flow so people would be healed and delivered, and His Name would be glorified. In prayer, He began to show me there was a connection to forgiveness and the release and reception of His power. He spoke to me this phrase again, *Faith pleases God, but forgiveness releases His power.* I began to ponder and meditate on this revelation. I wasn't enlightened to its full meaning. *Lord, show me please,* I prayed.

One day as I sat in my office at church talking on the phone, a lady knocked on the office door. She was a sales-person for television ads. I motioned for her to sit down and told her I would be off the phone in a minute. Before I hung up the phone, the Holy Spirit spoke to me saying, "She has unforgiveness." I ended the conversation on the phone and without introducing myself, I boldly stated, "God has told me you have unforgiveness in your heart."

She immediately started crying, and I took her hands and prayed with her to forgive whoever hurt her. The minute she forgave the people she had a grudge against, she started shouting that her hands were healed. I hadn't prayed for healing, nor did I know she had problems in her hands. She turned out to be a pastor's wife, and the people of their church were treating her husband wrongly, so she was harboring bitterness and unforgiveness. She had started having severe pain in her forearms and hands. She couldn't open and close her hands without severe pain. The minute she forgave, the tormenting pain left. She forgave, and God's power drove away the tormenting spirits and healed her. I later prayed for her husband, and we became good friends.

Prior to receiving this revelation connecting forgiving with praying for healing, the success in praying for people was about 30 to 35 percent. Now it was increasing greatly. All the glory to God! Ask and you shall receive.

# The Deaf Ear

There seemed to be more people not healed than healed before, but I was determined that healing was for today. I had seen it overseas, and I knew God loved people here as much as overseas. Maybe this forgiving, releasing power was a key.

I came up to a man in a prayer line, and he boldly told me a story of how 12 years before he had a bad inner ear infection and the doctors had removed all of his inner ear: eardrum, anvil, stirrup, everything. He had been totally deaf for 12 years in that ear. He proclaimed that God told Him that today he would be healed. He was excited. He appeared to have great faith. I figured this was going to be an easy miracle, and the rest of the people would have their faith raised to a higher level.

I prayed three times, and nothing happened. I told him to keep faith and simply believe. I started praying for other people, and they were being healed. All of a sudden, the Holy Spirit spoke to me and said he had hatred and unforgiveness in him. I turned back to him and stated that God had told me He had unforgiveness. He immediately fell to his knees and started crying. He began to share with me that he hated his old pastor because he had embarrassed him. I prayed with him to forgive and release him. He did. I prayed again for His ear. And praise God! The Lord did a creative miracle and restored everything that had been removed, and he heard perfectly. Once again, forgiveness was given and God's power was released.

Let's go to God's Word to confirm everything I am sharing with you. One day while reading His Word I saw that the Spirit who forgave sins was the same Spirit who healed.

*And, behold, they brought to Him a man sick of the palsy, lying on a bed: and Jesus seeing their faith said unto the sick of the palsy; Son, be of good cheer; thy sins be forgiven thee. And, behold, certain of the scribes said within themselves, This man blasphemeth. And Jesus knowing their thoughts said, Wherefore think ye evil in your hearts? For whether is easier, to say, Thy sins be forgiven thee; or to say, Arise, and walk? But that ye may know that the Son of man hath power on earth to forgive sins, (then saith He to the sick of the palsy,) Arise, take up thy bed, and go unto thine house. And he arose, and departed to his house* (Matthew 9:2-7).

The Holy Spirit showed me that His grace forgives and heals, and that what would hinder forgiveness would also hinder healing. Let's go to another passage about forgiveness.

*Therefore I say unto you, What things soever ye desire, when ye pray, believe that ye receive them, and ye shall have them. And when ye stand praying, forgive, if ye have ought against any: that your Father also which is in heaven may forgive you your trespasses. But if ye do not forgive, neither will your Father which is in heaven forgive your trespasses* (Mark 11:24-26).

It wasn't until after the Fall in the Garden that sin and sickness entered into the world. The Lord provided one medicine, one vaccine, for both, and I believe it is God's grace and forgiveness. In the above Scripture, we see if you don't forgive, it blocks you being forgiven. If you don't forgive, it will block your healing. About the same time the Holy Spirit gave me this revelation, I had just finished a long water-only fast that He had instructed me to do after returning from a trip from Africa. I believe that the fast was intended to restore what had been stolen from us in the ministry. I call this a dominion fast, which is very similar to Jesus' 40-day fast. Humankind had lost dominion of the earth, so His 40-day fast began to take dominion back. Humankind lost by eating in the Garden and Jesus reclaimed by not eating. Think about it.

This fast also removed doubt in our ministry so we could move ahead with this revelation of the power of forgiveness. We need to understand that forgiveness removes:

- Shame
- Condemnation
- Guilt
- Sin
- Sickness and disease

Forgiveness is the doorway to the supernatural. It releases God's power for salvation, healing, and deliverance. If you get anything out of this book, please learn that forgiveness isn't just something that we receive; it is the basis of what we preach, teach, and walk. We must not only *receive*, but live a life of *giving* forgiveness. We must intercede that forgiveness is released from Heaven to earth and on all those who are infected with the sin disease who have not been vaccinated by His grace.

We are about to get to the Scripture that holds I believe the main revelation to people being healed, delivered, and set free from demonic bondages.

*Then came Peter to Him, and said, Lord, how oft shall my brother sin against me, and I forgive him? till seven times? Jesus saith unto him, I say not unto thee, Until seven times: but, Until seventy times seven* [490 times a day].

*Therefore is the kingdom of heaven likened unto a certain king, which would take account of his servants. And when he had begun to reckon, one was brought unto him, which owed him ten thousand talents. But forasmuch as he had not to pay, his lord commanded him to be sold, and his wife, and children, and all that he had, and payment to be made.*

*The servant therefore fell down, and worshipped him, saying, Lord, have patience with me, and I will pay thee all. Then the lord of that servant was moved with compassion, and loosed him, and forgave him the debt.*

*But the same servant went out, and found one of his fellowservants, which owed him an hundred pence: and he laid hands on him, and took him by the throat, saying, Pay me that thou owest.*

*And his fellowservant fell down at his feet, and besought him, saying, Have patience with me, and I will pay thee all.*

*And he would not: but went and cast him into prison, till he should pay the debt. So when his fellowservants saw what was done, they were very sorry, and came and told unto their lord all that was done.*

*Then his lord, after that he had called him, said unto him, O thou wicked servant, I forgave thee all that debt, because thou desiredst me: Shouldest not thou also have had compassion on thy fellowservant, even as I had pity on thee? And his lord was wroth, and delivered him to the tormentors, till he should pay all that was due unto him.*

*So likewise shall My heavenly Father do also unto you, if ye from your hearts forgive not every one his brother their trespasses* (Matthew 18:21-35).

People always want grace and forgiveness when it comes to their own problems, but we find it hard to grant it to others who have wronged us or our loved ones. We might even mouth the words, trying to be obedient to the Lord, but He knows if the decision has been made in our heart or if we have only said the words. I encourage you to ask the Holy Spirit to assist you in making a conscious decision to surrender your wounded, hardened, bitter heart to Him so He can heal it. Then, and only then, can the tormentors be made to leave. Slowly, the enemy uses human puppets to offend, hurt, and cause bitterness. He knows that hurt people hurt people. But God knows healed people heal people.

We must understand that no one can heal except through the Name of Jesus Christ of Nazareth. His finished work on Calvary, His death and resurrection, changed everything. When He was tied to the whipping post before He was crucified, they severely beat Him. Remember, while there, and again later at the cross, He could have called ten thousand angels and shut the whole thing down, but He didn't. Praise God, because by those very stripes He received as He was tied to that post, mental, physical, and spiritual healing is available in His Name. His blood shed at the cross forgives sin.

## An Impossible Debt

In the previous pages, we read the parable of the man forgiven who wouldn't forgive. The Holy Spirit began to explain to me that in His Kingdom, people can only become citizens if they have been forgiven. Their citizenship depends on whether they have been touched by God's love and then filled with His love. God has empowered us with a fuel called love—not an earthly love of conditions, but a heavenly love that is unconditional. His love never fails. Our fuel source is an unfailing power that, when released, will always grant forgiveness and acceptance. Sometimes we forgive, but not accept. Yes, I know that there are times when we can't continue a relationship with people, such as in situations of rape, murder, and other abuse. We still need to forgive to keep in compliance with Kingdom principles. God's love really can't be explained totally. It's where someone will lay down his or her life for someone who doesn't deserve it. Like Jesus did for me.

The parable of the servant who owed the lord and couldn't pay is speaking of you and me owing a debt we couldn't pay, and He has excused us, pardoned us. He paid a debt He didn't owe. Now this same servant went out after having the lord graciously forgive and clear him of all debt. Not only forgiven, but debt-free. All things that used to be held against him were gone.

*Brethren, I count not myself to have apprehended: but this one thing I do, forgetting those things which are behind, and reaching forth unto those things which are before, I press toward the mark for the prize of the high calling of God in Christ Jesus* (Philippians 3:13-14).

Now having his slate cleared, he went out and dealt with someone who owed him and refused to show grace and mercy. Refusing to forgive, his heart was judged as wicked by his lord. He called him a wicked servant. He was called a servant, not a son. A servant doesn't walk in the Father's love and forgiveness. He doesn't represent the house as a son of the house does.

We've been adopted and forgiven. It is required of us to represent the Heavenly Father. Therefore, we are to walk in grace and mercy, forgiving all who ask for or desire this grace. I'm convinced it takes walking in the Spirit of grace to give grace. The Bible tells us God would meet us at the mercy seat to talk to us. If He, being perfect, meets us and deals with us at the mercy seat, how much more do we need to receive grace and mercy each morning before dealing with people? After being judged wicked, this person was turned over to the tormentors, and then Jesus tells his listeners, "So will your heavenly Father do unto you." Immediately when I heard the word "tormentors," this Scripture came to my mind:

> *There is no fear in love; but perfect love casteth out fear: because **fear hath torment**. He that feareth is not made perfect in love* (1 John 4:18).

Refusing to forgive would cause this judgment of having tormenting spirits loosed on us. The Bible tells us that fear is a spirit. Second Timothy 1:7 says, *"For God hath not given us the spirit of fear, but of power, and of love, and of a sound mind."*

I came to the conclusion that tormenting spirits could be the problem with people experiencing fear and phobia. I even came to believe that sickness and disease that doctors couldn't cure were tormentors given room through unforgiveness or fear given place through traumatic situations. I believe that the Holy Ghost was revealing this to me and decided that if this is God then I will apply it in prayer lines and in counseling situations. It started slowly at first, but it has taken healing percentages in our ministry from 35 to 75 percent. That's amazing.

# Truly Free

Read about this lady and how God set her free. We had only had the church in Parkersburg going for about a year. There was this doctor who kept referring his patients to come to our church if they really wanted to get healed.

I received a call from him about this lady with severe phobias of crowds, people, and being in public. She hadn't left her house in two years except to go to the doctor, and then she would close her eyes until she got there and close them before she would leave until she got home. She kept her blinds closed and lights on dim. I called her and she said I could come over. I had a woman from the church meet me there and after talking to her, found out that her ex-husband had abused her, beat her, walked out on her. Since he had left, she had been in mental hospitals six times, lost her driver's license because of seizures, lost her job, and was on total disability. Now she was tormented in this prison of fear.

I told her about forgiveness and how it worked and that she could be set free if she forgave. She needed to do it for herself and for Christ's sake. With much prompting and gentle encouragement, she managed to pray with us. She was crying and sobbing uncontrollably. Once she forgave her ex-husband, a peace came on her face and she quietly wept, thanking the Lord.

That night she actually came to church. It had been two years in her home as a literal prison. She was a little nervous, but she came. I was so proud of her and thankful to the Lord. Two days later, she called my cell phone. She was screaming. I had to tell her to speak calmly so I could understand. She then told me she was in Wal-Mart, and there were many people. She wasn't afraid and she was witnessing about her miracle and inviting people to church. She forgave, and the spirits of torment now had no legal ground to be there. To God be all the glory for showing us these keys to the Kingdom.

We have seen so many phobias, sicknesses, and mental torments healed instantly after forgiving people of their past who had hurt them or done them wrong. Yours may be:

- Ex-husband/ex-wife
- First boyfriend/girlfriend
- School teacher
- Coach
- Parents/grandparents
- Pastors/ church people
- Boss/co-worker
- Or perhaps a criminal who victimized you

Whatever your traumatic experience or hurt might have been—someone lied, betrayed, or ridiculed you—your unforgiveness opens a door to torment. We have seen arthritis, bursitis, and fibromyalgia healed. We have seen paralysis leave. We have also seen unforgiveness deafen ears, blind eyes, and cripple legs. Many have been prayed for by big-name ministries. But once they forgave from their hearts, not just their lips, they received their healing.

I realized you can't be forgiven if you don't forgive, so I started praying before the salvation prayer and healing prayer that people would forgive others, themselves, and even God. I have seen so many people come to church and then disappear. They answered altar calls and prayed the sinner's prayer, but it seemed as if there would not be any change in their lives. I wanted to see real Holy Ghost change where evil, wicked hearts would be turned to soft hearts that were gentle, loving, and forgiving. I am continuing to do this today, having people pray and forgive all offenders before they pray the sinner's prayer or a healing prayer. Now I've been around long enough to know that they must be educated on the fact, so I take a few minutes and teach on the hindrance of having unforgiveness.

Remember, *faith moves God, but forgiveness releases God's power.* At the same time, unforgiveness releases or gives room to satan's power. I cannot count the people whose lives have been changed by this message—hundreds, even thousands. I have preached on forgiveness in countries such as South Africa, Nicaragua, and Costa Rica. I have preached at many Native American reservations. Whether it was African Americans, Latinos, Caucasians, American Indians, Pakistanis, or other races—no matter who, Jesus died for all and has made provision for all to be forgiven and to have power to forgive. Salvation includes forgiveness, healing, deliverance, and prosperity—to be made whole of our afflictions. Everything that was lost to humankind has been redeemed at Calvary by the unselfish death of Jesus Christ. In the court of Heaven, it has been recorded that forgiveness and restoration to the Father is available for every person who will heed the call from His throne. It is for everyone who will answer God's heart cry to forgive and be forgiven.

We must be born again. We must allow ourselves to be healed and delivered. I want to take some time to share some testimonies of people of different races, cultures, and economic situations. As they forgave and received forgiveness, they were healed.

# Healing Testimonies

The following testimonies are from men and women who were previously tormented mentally or physically, with chronic pain, anxiety, sickness, or disease, who prayed to make a conscious decision to forgive, and have seen God's power released for their healing.

*Special note:* We give all the credit and glory to Jesus for all healings. Only Jesus saves and heals.

### Kimberly from Alabama

Praise to our God! It is with joy and thankfulness that I am writing this message to you. I have suffered with psoriatic arthritis for almost five years. Almost five years ago I began developing a myriad of physical symptoms: extreme fatigue, horrible joint pain, a rash on one of my legs, nausea, weight loss, profound anemia, my hands and lips would turn blue, as well as other symptoms. After two years, having seen ten doctors, I was diagnosed with psoriatic arthritis. No cure (the world's opinion) and the meds to control the disease are laden with side effects. I had no quality of life and was no longer able to work as a registered nurse. I had days where just walking across a room would take my breath away.

My emotional life was just as difficult. My husband and I did not get along, and we were trying to raise our four-year-old daughter. Through these years I became so tormented in my thoughts; I was bitter, angry, sick all the time, and could not believe that people would treat me the way that they did. This included my husband, our kids, my family, my in-laws, everyone. All the while I would attend church, smile in public, and even read my Bible.

I assumed that everyone else needed to change. I would ask God to help, but the longer things went on, the more distant He became to me. Some months ago I began to have thoughts about forgiveness. I would hear teachers talk about it and even made a sticky note for my computer to remind me about being a forgiving person. I didn't get it though. Two months ago I saw you, Dr. Adams, on television. I listened, and my spirit finally heard words of hope. I ordered your series and began listening to the CDs. I don't know exactly which CD or which prayer it may have been, but *I got it!* I have been delivered, transformed, and healed of my arthritis! Praise God! I have energy and a happy heart. Just last week I was able to travel with my husband and little girl on a business trip for the first time. I took her to a farm and walked without pain or stiffness. I was able to crouch down and watch tadpoles in a pond for some time. I stood up and began walking. It was at that moment that I realized that the arthritis was completely gone. Before, if I had been able to crouch down at all, I would have had to get on my hands and knees and struggle to get up, then deal with the pain until I could move again. *No longer!*

My husband even tells me that my appearance has changed; people tell me that they hear it in my voice. My relationship with my husband has been restored! When God transforms you, when you are obedient, nothing will stop the impact it will have, not only on you, but also on those around you. I am continuing to listen to the series and working on taking every thought captive and praying constant forgiveness. I know that by His grace I will do it. There is more to my story; the Lord is still working, and I am ready to tell all of what the Lord has done and is doing in my life.

Thank you, Dr. Adams, for being obedient, for listening to the Holy Spirit, and for sharing God's revelation. Accepting Christ was the most important thing I have ever done, learning to forgive is right beside it and completes the work of the cross in my life. May God bless you, your family, and your church. I want everyone to hear this message. I excitedly look forward to sharing even more of God's wondrous works.

## Jill from Ohio

Despite heavy medication, I suffered from chronic pain in my shoulders and other complications for 11 years. The pain was intolerable.

My husband is from India, and his sister who lives there had seen Pastor Brian Adams on the Sid Roth show *It's Supernatural* and asked us to visit the church which is within two hours of our home.

We visited The Rock with great hope and expectancy to receive a miracle from our Lord Jesus with Pastor Brian Adams as the chosen vessel and the church as His chosen place. I received my miracle. I am finally pain free. I thank God for His grace, love, and mercy. He has truly redeemed me from destruction.

I thank God and the ministry of Pastor Brian and the church family for being there for me. I encourage everyone seeking a healing miracle to get in touch with this ministry in submission to Jesus Christ and expect a miracle. *Praise the Lord!*

## Kelly from Ohio

Pastor Brian came to West Virginia on March 5, 2011. I had pain in my neck and jaw. My sinuses were blocked. Pastor Brian prayed for me. I woke up the next morning pain free. Two days later there was no more sinus pressure or drainage. I was completely healed. Thank You, Jesus.

## Sue from Texas

Over the phone with Dr. Adams, I was instantly delivered from depression, anxiety, and a hearing problem in my right ear. I was also prayed for my eyesight. I am now believing for 20/20 vision.

## Rev. Collins from Colorado

Dr. Adams was in Denver, Colorado ministering at our church. Many were healed in the meeting. My sister in Tulsa, Oklahoma had 70 percent loss of hearing in both ears. Dr. Adams prayed for her over the phone, and God healed her. She is hearing fine now. Thank God for Dr. Adams.

## Esther from Ohio

My husband and I moved here from Florida a year and a half ago. In Florida on December 28, 2007, I was told that I had stage four breast cancer and that it had already spread through my entire body. They gave me 6 months to live and a 30 percent chance of making it to 3 years. We felt that God had told us to move back home, but I hesitated because I didn't want my family to think I was moving home to die. God's Word said I was healed and that I will live a long life. I believed God's report, not the doctor's. We looked for a church where the pastors preached the Word of God and believed in healing. In March of 2010 we found The Rock in Jackson, Ohio, with pastors who connected with us through the Word.

The very first night we were there, Pastor Brian prayed the prayer of agreement with me that I was healed and would live and not die. That was a blessing in itself. Not too many pastors would pray that prayer in faith and not back off. Shortly after that, the doctors told me I had several tumors in the membrane around my brain, and they did radiation therapy. They didn't think it would do much good. Pastor Brian once again in faith prayed for a miracle for me. After the radiation treatments were done, the doctors did an MRI. They waited two months because the doctor said it would tell more. I went in for my report and my doctor came in and grabbed me and danced me around, praising the Lord and calling me her miracle patient. The MRI came back perfect, better than she had even hoped for. A few months later I had to go in for my check ups and another MRI. All reports came back perfect; the doctors were thrilled. This past December 2010 was the three year mark that we celebrated. God is good and faithful to keep His Word. He is more than able to do what He promised. It is a blessing to have a pastor who is not afraid to pray the Word of God over you. The prayers of the pastor and the people at the church have been a great encouragement to me and many others. All praise to God and the pastors He placed in the Body of Christ. We are blessed.

## Deanna from Missouri

Pastor Brian prayed for my son and daughter. My son had some type of tumor growing in his back. He was scheduled for an MRI four days after he was prayed over, and there is not a sign of anything in his back. My daughter had a low white blood cell count and was not gaining weight. She put on a pound and half before her next appointment and her blood count is perfect. They are no longer worried about her weight. She is doing just fine now. Pastor Brian's preaching has really helped me focus my life in the right direction.

## Kimberly from Illinois

Pastor Brian visited our church in Illinois, and God used him to speak into my life powerfully. I was battling some offenses and hurt within myself and wasn't sure exactly how to deal with them. I knew it was hurting me and the church because the offenses and hurt had come from a leadership member. God healed my heart in many ways those couple of days, and the last night, God spoke words to me that I needed to hear for so long. I felt like I was being corrected and loved all at the same time and I received it and allowed those words to change me right then, healing areas that I thought would never be healed. I know true renewal happened, and I am so thankful for God loving me enough to send someone to speak to me when I needed it most. Thank You, Jesus!

## Sheila from the U.S.A.

When our pastor asked for Pastor Brian to come, many in the church were excited. Pastor Troy had been in the church a few days before that with Pastor Brian. The Holy Spirit filled our church service so strong the other evening, I asked Pastor Brian to pray for my feet to be healed from the pain I have carried for a long time. He did. Quickly the pain went away. All I could say was, "It's true! It's true!" Then I started running with no more pain. Thank You, Jesus. Praise the Lord. God is good all the time.

## Cole Oakley from Ohio

I was diagnosed with Torsion Dystonia. This was brought on by a football injury. I suffered for over 100 days. I had to wear a sling for my right arm. My entire right side was crippled. This is such a rare disorder that there are only four known cases in the entire world, three of which are in Africa. After Pastor Brian prayed for me, the pain left, and I was able to stand up straight. The doctor said this was incurable. My family and I had given up hope and didn't know what to do. I walked out pain free without the sling and standing totally erect! I give God all the praise!

## Deanna from the U.S.A.

I had severe pain in my leg and hip. I would have to walk with a cane. After Dr. Brian prayed for me, my leg was better and I was able to walk without the cane. The pain had completely left.

## Marilyn from New Mexico

I had glaucoma and my vision was diminishing. After prayer, I could immediately see better. The following day I went to the eye doctor and I no longer have glaucoma. Thank You, Jesus!

## Carol from New Mexico, Navajo Nation

I was on oxygen and had breathing problems due to asthma. When I was prayed for, I was able to breathe with ease and without my oxygen. Praise the Lord.

## Rosemary from New Mexico, Navajo Nation

I had pain in my back, legs, and knees due to arthritis. After receiving prayer, the pain left and I can bend and move. Thank You, Jesus.

## Lucinda from Navajo Nation

I suffered severe pain in my hands for years. I couldn't open and close them. When Pastor Brian prayed for me, the pain immediately left and my hands and fingers move freely. I am finally healed.

## Katherine from New Mexico, Navajo Nation

My whole body has been in pain for years. Feet, hips, back, and all my bones hurt all the time. Doctors could not find the problem. I had to be helped down to the altar. When he prayed for me, I felt warm and tingly all over. The pain has left and I can walk without help. God is truly awesome.

## Christine from New Mexico, Navajo Nation

I had severe pain in the left side of my chest from cancer. I had chemotherapy today and felt weak. After prayer, the pain is totally gone and I feel much stronger.

## Nicole from Navajo Nation

My right ear had loss of hearing and my upper left arm has been hurting. The pastor prayed for me, and the pain left my arm and my ear is completely open.

## Emily from New Mexico, Navajo Nation

I had asthma and a heart murmur. After prayer, I could feel it beating right, and I can breathe much better. Thank the Lord.

## Evelyn from Arizona, Navajo Nation

My fingers were bent closed and hurting. I could not open and extend them. After prayer they are now opening and closing freely without pain. Praise the Lord.

## Christina from New Mexico, Navajo Nation

I could not hear out of my ear for four or five days. Now I can hear perfectly after receiving prayer. Thank You, Jesus.

## William from New Mexico, Navajo Nation

Once I would sit for a long time, I could not walk because of the pain where my back had gone out. I also had around 70 percent hearing loss in both ears. After receiving prayer from the pastor, I could sit and stand or walk without pain and my ears are totally opened. Thank God for His miracle power.

## Delbert from New Mexico, Navajo Nation

I had pain very bad in my legs and walked into the service with a cane. After being prayed for, all pain was gone and I walked out without a cane.

## Lisa from Vienna, West Virginia

I had pain in my shoulder for six years, and now the pain is gone due to prayer. Praise the Lord.

## Deanna from West Virginia

I had fibromyalgia and pain in my back and leg. I am now healed. Thank you for praying for me. God is real.

## Geri from West Virginia

When I was prayed for, Jesus healed my back and took the ringing out of my ears. Praise the Lord.

## Jeanne from Ohio

I was missing cartilage in my knee and had severe pain. I received healing, and the pain is totally gone. Thank You, Jesus, for replacing the cartilage in my knee.

## Wayne from West Virginia

Both of my knees had the cartilage missing and I walked with a lot of pain. When Pastor Brian prayed for me, Jesus healed me, and now I walk normally with no pain.

## Eleanor from New Mexico, Navajo Nation

I was born with no eardrum in my left ear. I am 64 years old, and in a meeting on the reservation, Pastor Brian prayed for me and I now hear 100 percent. Sixty-four years of silence, and now I can hear perfect in that ear. Thank You, Jesus!

## Melissa from Ohio

My son, Jeremiah, was born May 13, 2008. When he was born, he was stillborn. He had no life to him at all for about 12 minutes. God brought him back and gave him life. Two weeks later the doctor came in and told me he was completely blind. The doctors told me that we should be very thankful that our son made it. They also said that he had really bad apnea, RDS, and hypertension. I told that doctor I know that he is going to make it, because God brought him back to life and He is not done with him yet. I then started coming to Pastor Brian's church, and they started praying for his blindness. I took him back to the eye doctor and the doctor said he could see completely. I know God is real, and He is a healer. God can do anything. You just have to believe.

## Karen from West Virginia

I had been troubled with periodic episodes of vertigo for many years. I told my doctor, and he sent me to a specialist. I got worse and had attacks daily while

THE POWER OF FORGIVENESS

on vacation. They ran tests, and during the testing, I went to The Rock and Pastor Brian prayed for me. I've had no vertigo at all since, and the specialist found nothing: no tumors, cysts, or other problems. He made up a diagnosis just to have something to say and dismissed me. Thank God and Brian for calling me out; I'm a bit quiet in church, but God knows who we are and what our problems are without us telling anyone.

No fireworks or dramatic stuff, just the awesome goodness and love of God came over me and healed me! I felt wrapped in a blanket, wow! We serve an awesome God!

## Nikki Bledsoe from Ohio

In 1998 after a stressful day, I went home to soak in a bubble bath. This time, however, the pressure of the water burst a hole in my eardrum. I went to a specialist who built a new lining, but assured me I would never regain hearing in that ear again. But in 2007 the Lord had other plans. I heard an awesome service on healing as Pastor Brian ministered, which encouraged me to have a leap of faith, trust God's Word, and believe that He still performs those miracles today. I'm glad I did. After praying over my ear, instantly I regained 100 percent of my hearing back which is still there today. I then learned that God really does unconditionally love each of us individually, and we are to love each other the same way. That part was a little harder to learn. I asked the Lord to show me how to do that and where to start. He revealed to me that I was missing love because I let all the times I have been hurt in the past make me bitter, feeling alone and rejected. I then saw how Jesus will never leave us feeling rejected, alone, or unloved. Then He reached down and turned my stony heart into a heart of flesh again! It felt like my heart had been ripped out and thrown into fire. I knew He was definitely doing something! I have been told how dramatically I had changed not long after that. My only response: God's love is awesome, and He's got enough love for you too!

## James from Ohio

I am 72 years old and I had bulging discs and arthritis. The doctors said they could do nothing for me. I had gone from a cane to a walker, and was very soon going to a wheelchair. I had been eight years walking with some type of assistance, and very slowly at that. I also had high blood pressure which caused ringing in my ears. When Pastor Brian prayed for me, I felt the Holy Ghost like never before. I started vibrating all over, and my back and knees were very hot. After the vibrating stopped, I got up and ran around the church completely healed of all pain and ringing in my ears. I feel young again. My wife carried my walker out and I walked out by myself standing straight up. Praise the Lord!

## Jessie from Ohio

I had what is called Barrett's disease. It causes erosion of the esophagus which is accompanied by constant coughing. When prayed for, I felt an uncontrollable trembling throughout my body. My pain left and my coughing has stopped. Thank you, Jesus!

## Dennis from West Virginia

Nearly 20 years ago, I severely damaged my knees through the wear and tear of downhill skiing for many years. Over the past five years the pain had increased to the point of daily experiencing pain from the most basic activities such as climbing stairs or walking at a fast pace.

On Saturday evening, Brian Adams prayed for my knees and I felt the power of God flow through my joints. The best way I can describe the experience is that it felt like warm gel poured over my legs. Within minutes I no longer felt any pain! I jumped and kneeled, and I felt like I was 20 years old again. Praise God, I am healed.

## Peggy from Ohio

I had a stroke, and it left my right leg shorter than my left. Pastor Brian prayed and my legs are now the same size. I feel so much better when I walk. I praise God for healing me, and for the wisdom, healing gift, caring, and time for others that Pastor Brian shares so freely.

## Pastor Patterson from Ohio

At age 74, he was diagnosed with prostate cancer and had lost 20 pounds. He was very weak and tired and had problems eating. His prostate cancer (PSA) count had risen to 487.00, and after having prayer at the church in my office, he returned two weeks later and had put on 20 pounds and his PSA count is now 1.3. The doctors told him this was impossible. He is now healed. To God be the glory!

## Brenda from Ohio

I met Pastor Brian at a funeral of a friend. He asked if he could pray for me. I was healed of hearing loss and fibromyalgia which I had had for ten years. At another time I had a frozen shoulder and couldn't raise my arm, and I was also healed. I thank God for sending this true man of faith into our lives!

## Shannon from Texas

I had a stroke and had lost 50 percent use of my left arm. I could only get ten pounds of pressure when I squeezed something. When he prayed for me, I was totally healed with total use of my arm and I gave my heart to the Lord. I feel awesome!

## Nicole from Texas

I broke my hand and it had been three weeks. The doctor said it would take six weeks to heal. Pastor Brian prayed for me and the pain left. The next day at the doctor, he said it was healed totally. Praise God!

## Rev. Taylor from Texas

I was delivered from strong hate and unforgiveness toward people who hurt me. Once I forgave, I was healed of heart arrhythmia and diabetes. Thank You, God!

## Ether from Texas

I had a hard time walking because of pain in my back and legs. The Pastor prayed for me and the pain is gone.

## LaShana from Texas

I was healed from fibromyalgia. Thank You, Jesus!

## Stella from Ohio

I came to visit The Rock in Jackson and I was a mess. I was suffering from depression and was deaf in my right ear and 70 percent deaf in my left ear. My right hand was broken and swollen, and I had not seen a doctor because of finances. Pastor Brian prayed for my hand and the pain left immediately and so did the swelling; it was healed right on the spot. He then prayed for my ears and they were also healed right then. I accepted the Lord as my Savior and the depression immediately left. Thank You, Jesus, for everything.

## Eddie from California

I was born again and delivered from unforgiveness, anger, insecurities, and pornography.

## Dave from California

I had 70 percent hearing loss in both ears, plus ringing in addition to neck and back pain. My hearing was totally restored and pain is completely gone.

## Lloyce from California

My neck and back pain was totally healed.

## Emilio from California

A car wreck left him with brain damage. He couldn't move legs, hands, or neck and only had limited arm movement. He made no eye contact and had limited concentration and speech. Pastor Brian prayed for him, and he stated moving his neck, looking at people, and moving his legs and arms. Praise God!

## LaShawn from California

I had a lumbar laminectomy with spinal fusion and metal hardware which keeps me in pain and restricts me from bending or turning. I could not even lift my legs. Pastor Brian prayed for me and all pain left. Now I can bend, twist, and lift my legs. I'm as good as I was before I was hurt. Thank You, Jesus!

### Crystal from California

I was delivered from fear, oppression, and condemnation. I was tormented by these most of my life. I am now free!

### Mattie from California

I was healed from severe back problems.

### Crystal from California

I was healed of fibromyalgia, spinal stenosis, neck and back pain, bulging discs, and arthritis in the knees. Praise God!

### Daryl from California

The retina separation in my right eye was healed. Thank You, Jesus!

### Rosae from California

I fell and injured my knee and needed an operation. Now the pain is all gone; I'm healed.

### Sophia from California

I was prayed for poor vision and my vision has been restored. Yes!

### Guy from Missouri

In March, 2007 in Missouri, Pastor Brian prayed for my healing. My heart had been damaged and only had about 21 percent ejection fraction due to an electrical malfunction in the left ventricle. I was healed when Pastor Brian prayed. We returned home that weekend and went to the cardiologist on Tuesday for a prearranged appointment for an echocardiogram. My heart no longer had an electrical problem. All of my heart was beating in synchronization where it had not done so before.

## Josefina

I am 42 years old. About two years ago, I had an accident at work. I fell down the stairs, and the following week had to have surgery on my knee. The doctors informed me that I would no longer be able to walk or run without a brace. While Dr. Brian Adams was having a revival service at the church I attend, I went to the front to have him pray and ask God to heal my knee. He prayed for my knee and asked me to stand up and do something I haven't been able to do. He told me to run down the aisle and back. At first I was hesitant but I said OK. I ran down the aisle and back with absolutely no pain. I have been healed.

## Eddie from the U.S.A.

After an endoscopy procedure done on my esophagus and stomach, my doctor was not happy about the results. Expecting to find a bacterial infection in my stomach which could be easily treated, instead, he found a possible cancer of the intestines. This seemed to be the probable answer with a terminal outcome. I refused to have the next test done until I could get to church for prayer. Well, the Lord sent Brian Adams into my life. He prayed over me, and the presence of the Holy Spirit was so strong. Something certainly did happen inside my stomach. It was jerking and rolling all at the same time. I read, listened to tapes, and repeated healing Scriptures day after day and even in the night prior to the next test. The day I was to go for the results, I felt the Lord tell me He had given me my miracle. When the doctor walked into the exam room, he was rubbing his hands together and smiling. He said, "I cannot explain it, but your tests are in normal limits." We thank the Lord for getting to meet you and we pray for you and your ministry.

## Tracie from the U.S.A.

I was diagnosed with bipolar depression with split personality disorder. I heard voices in my head, and there wasn't ever a moment of peace. I was a walking time bomb. I had severe emotional trauma due to childhood abuse, neglect, and rejection which planted many bitter roots in my soul and opened the door for the enemy to attack me. Brian Adams preached at a revival in my church, and on the last day I felt the urge to answer an altar call. The minute Brian's hand touched my head, the voices stopped. All glory to God and many thanks for answered prayer.

*Chapter 7*

# HARVESTING TOOL

As long as our eyes are upon ourselves and our feelings and emotions, we take ourselves out of Kingdom business. It's time to win souls and bring them into the Kingdom of God. God's Word tells us that the Lord doesn't want any to be lost.

*For the Son of man is come to save that which was lost* (Matthew 18:11).

*The Lord is not slack concerning His promise, as some men count slackness; but is longsuffering to us-ward, not willing that any should perish, but that all should come to repentance* (2 Peter 3:9).

We must be born again by Spirit and water. If we don't forgive, we can't be forgiven. His Word tells us to repent of all sins and be born again. Remember our saying: *Faith moves God, but forgiveness releases His power.* When His forgiveness is given, His power is released. His power is the Holy Ghost, the third person of the Trinity.

God's Word tells us that He, the Holy Ghost, convicts the world of their sins. When we forgive, and even ask God to forgive, the convicting power of God is loosed from Heaven and now the work has begun for this person's salvation.

*Whose soever sins ye remit, they are remitted unto them; and whose soever sins ye retain, they are retained* (John 20:23).

We have become disciples of Christ, and distributors of forgiveness. We are to teach it, preach it, walk it, live it, prophesy it, breathe it, and even die in its power. The grace of God, His forgiveness, becomes the atmosphere where miracles happen.

His anger has been appeased by the death of His Son. He has forgiven us and made it available to those who ask. We can also release it by intercession to the unsaved. Christ did it while on the cross. *"Father, forgive them; for they know not what they do..."* (Luke 23:34).

To truly walk in God's forgiveness, we must surrender to God's Spirit totally, for it takes the supernatural love of God to forgive the way He wants us to. God's love isn't a conditional love. It is unconditional. He loved while we were still sinners, and He continues to love us. Remember, none of us deserved to be forgiven by God. It is the love and grace of God which forgives us. Once we receive this, we have it to give to others.

The Word tells us that one who has been forgiven much loves much. True forgiveness happens when we repent of our sins, when we stop doing wrong. Being forgiven releases the power of God to break the power of sin. When this happens and we leave the prison of sin, we rejoice and then want to tell others so we can see others experience this same power. It is our obligation to inform others of this awesome forgiveness that God has made available to all who accept Him.

Forgiveness from God isn't a one-time event, His mercy is renewed daily.

*If we confess our sins, He is faithful and just to forgive us our sins, and to cleanse us from all unrighteousness* (1 John 1:9).

Only through Christ can we go to the Father, and only His love can release His forgiveness. His forgiveness releases His power to heal, deliver, and transform. People cannot get saved on their own. There must be people crying out that God forgive them and save them from their sins. If we demand justice for people when we are angry at them, we imprison them in their sins. This isn't God's will. We are God's agents on earth to request, as Christ has done, that they be forgiven.

The effect of forgiveness is the most powerful tool of evangelism known to man. When we have been forgiven, and we understand that others' sin is due to ignorance, that they are being blinded by the god of this world, satan, we desire them to be released from his control and to become immersed in the love of God.

Even as I write this last chapter of this book on the harvest, I must be totally honest. I only understand this supernatural power to a small degree. It is a key, a tool, a principle of the Kingdom we truly need to begin to walk in. Every one of us is an able-bodied minister of reconciliation for God. We must preach that we can be forgiven by grace without works, that it is a gift. We then educate that once we receive forgiveness, we become employed to distribute what we have received.

I've always heard that you could catch more flies with honey than with vinegar. The Gospel of Christ is good news. Is what you are preaching good news to those who are hearing it? Are you being a heavenly message of glad tidings to the inhabitants of this earth?

You see, God is no longer angry at humankind. His anger has been appeased by the death of His Son Christ Jesus now that sin has had its price paid. The wages of sin is death and the price was paid by Jesus. What God has to give man now is good.

*Or despisest thou the riches of His goodness and forbearance and longsuffering; not knowing that the goodness of God leadeth thee to repentance?* (Romans 2:4)

We need to tell all men and women that they can be forgiven and receive their pardon from Heaven. Oh, this excites me every time I think, speak, or write about this topic.

*For God so loved the world, that He gave His only begotten Son, that whosoever believeth in Him should not perish, but have everlasting life* (John 3:16).

There must first be love from God. Human love is conditional. God's love is unconditional. Forgiveness is the fruit of love. Before fruit can grow there must be a Kingdom atmosphere of peace, righteousness, and joy. Jesus gave us a peace the world doesn't know. He gave us His righteousness, which we receive by faith. When we see our prayers answered, our joy is full.

In this heavenly atmosphere, His love through us, fertilized by our crucified flesh, produces this antidote called forgiveness. The act of forgiving one another actually lifts Christ up. It is like reliving the scene of Him on the cross of Calvary. We are enacting Christ being lifted up.

*And I, if I be lifted up from the earth, will draw all men unto Me* (John 12:32).

Let's pray to the Lord of this harvest that laborers will be sent into the harvest, laborers empowered with the power of forgiveness. If we don't read and study to show ourselves approved unto God, then we will not know how to properly respond to the storms and offenses that come against us. If we walk around with a chip on our shoulder, we will do the Kingdom more harm than good. If we have a posture of defending ourselves, we will repel instead of draw sinners.

## Receive to Give

Receiving forgiveness is one of the greatest answers to prayer. Our answered prayers release joy. The joy of the Lord is our strength. After times of repentance have come, times of refreshing, manifest joy, and being refreshed draw sinners to us. They begin to ask us why are we so happy. We simply answer we have been forgiven, redeemed, and pardoned. A substitute has taken our place and paid the price for our sins. We then make this same forgiveness available to them.

When we intercede and ask the Lord to forgive people, we hear ourselves talking about someone being forgiven. We remember our experience and it starts all over again—the joy, strength, times of refreshing, and the power from God flowing from us. We actually become a window between Heaven and earth from which the message of forgiveness can be preached, released, and distributed.

*Faith moves God, but forgiveness releases His power.* This power convicts, converts, breaks yokes, delivers, heals, and opens eyes and ears to see and hear from Heaven.

Forgiving is the nature, character, and even the personality of God. His mercy and grace is renewed every morning.

If we walk in the power of forgiveness, we will become powerful evangelists bringing souls to the glorious light of the Lord Jesus Christ. Forgiveness emanates health, happiness, and holiness from the Kingdom of God.

We must lay down our lives for the sake of our fellow brothers and sisters, as did Christ. We must become doers of the Word of God so His love will be perfected in us. As this love is perfected, fear will be cast out of us. We will then, without fear of dying, share this powerful Gospel message of forgiveness. We must tell the world that God is not angry at them and that He wants to forgive everyone and restore the "child to the Father" relationship (see Mal. 4:6).

We've been educated now that sin, hatred, and bitterness have blinded the eyes of people. We not only need to preach this message, we need to become intercessors for souls. Just as Christ on the cross, we need to ask God to forgive people for they know not what they are doing. The Scripture tells us that what we loose on earth is loosed in Heaven.

Let's look at Jesus. He forgave the man's sin who was let down through the roof, the woman who was caught in adultery, the man who had the withered hand, and many more. He loosed forgiveness on earth, and then prayed for it to be loosed by God in Heaven. Skilled soul-winners need to know these Kingdom secrets, mysteries kept hidden from the Church by the devil through religion. Jesus told us that we had the right to know the mysteries of Heaven.

*And the disciples came, and said unto Him, Why speakest Thou unto them in parables? He answered and said unto them, Because it is given unto you to know the mysteries of the kingdom of heaven, but to them it is not given* (Matthew 13:10-11).

The scribes and Pharisees had problems with a mere human being able to forgive sins here on earth. Christ has given us some of the power of remission of sins. Before you panic and think I'm talking heresy, let me explain. We can't get someone saved without their participation, but we can intercede and remit some sins. As we look at Scripture, remember the more sin a person bears, the more legal ground the devil has to hold on to him. By prayer and remission, we are working with God to relieve some pressure, so to speak, requesting God's Holy Spirit to intervene.

*Whose soever sins ye remit, they are remitted unto them; and whose soever sins ye retain, they are retained* (John 20:23).

Jesus knew He was returning to the Father, and the work of the harvest was only beginning. When He commissioned people to preach and heal, included in that preaching was prayer and remission.

*If any man see his brother sin a sin which is not unto death, he shall ask, and he shall give him life for them that sin not unto death. There is a sin unto death: I do not say that he shall pray for it* (1 John 5:16).

## Our Commission

We need to begin to remit people's sin in Jesus' Name and ask the Lord to forgive sins not unto death. Remember, when God's forgiveness is given, His power is released. Again, I will repeat myself. His power is none other than the third person of the Godhead, the Holy Ghost, who convicts us of our sins. Layers of the world's sin and the penalty of these sins begin to be peeled off, and the Holy Ghost can now begin to convict people and remove the blindness from their eyes where the god of this world has blinded them so they can't see their need for Christ.

This type of prayer and intercession for God the Father to have mercy and save is so powerful. We have been required to network with Heaven and then to be trained to become an ambassador of Christ, going forth, preaching and sharing God's love, becoming a distributor of the power of forgiveness.

You and I have the antidote to this second-death causing disease called sin. Heaven wants us to set up stations and offer this vaccine to cure this demonic plague which is running rampant. Hell has even opened and enlarged its mouth because so many have died in this condition. Someone must shout to this world, there is a Heaven to gain and a hell to shun. Who is this someone? It is you and I.

There is a great commission given by Christ from Heaven to us here on the earth. We must, as an army from Heaven, unselfishly take our part to tell people that not only do we need to be forgiven, but we need to forgive.

When Heaven hears our cry and prayer requesting forgiveness, not only for us but for others, then earth will experience a revival of God's power as never before. It will purge and cleanse humankind. Get ready—as you forgive, His power will be released.

# Chapter 8

# NOTE FROM KAREN'S HEART

As I sit pondering and meditating over the different seasons of my life, I believe that the simplicity of the Gospel is truly found in the act of forgiveness. Maybe the word *act* should be capitalized, because I believe for many it is just a *Fact* we want to talk about, but an *Act* we never have any intention of applying to our lives.

It talks big. It can make us sound so spiritual and loving. It seems to be actually what we all know we need to do as human beings, but the hardest thing that most of us will ever do. Why? Because it makes us vulnerable. According to what I read in the Scriptures, I can tell you this. Forgiveness is an issue that continues to pop up from Genesis to Revelation. It seems interlaced throughout each book of the Bible. The Book of Genesis begins with a perfect world only to end the last chapter with Joseph, who had the ultimate betrayal by his brothers, offering forgiveness to his family.

*And they sent a messenger unto Joseph, saying, Thy father did command before he died, saying, So shall ye say unto*

*Joseph, Forgive, I pray thee now, the trespass of thy brethren, and their sin; for they did unto thee evil: and now, we pray thee, forgive the trespass of the servants of the God of thy father. And Joseph wept when they spake unto him. And his brethren also went and fell down before his face; and they said, Behold, we be thy servants. And Joseph said unto them, Fear not: for am I in the place of God? But as for you, ye thought evil against me; but God meant it unto good, to bring to pass, as it is this day, to save much people alive* (Genesis 50:16-20).

Many years ago, I read a devotional article written by a woman who had a very young granddaughter who had been brutally raped and murdered. She cried out to God, inquiring as to how she was ever going to forgive this man who had been so merciless to her grandchild. She knew as a Christian woman that, unless she could forgive him, she could not be forgiven. Yet the crime had reached so deep into her being that she did not know how she was going to release this man. As she sought the Lord in prayer, the Lord spoke to her and said, "Don't look at the *deed* done. Look at the *need* this man has to be forgiven." Wow! What a key to forgiveness the Lord revealed to this grief-stricken grandmother.

I have pondered this story many times over the years as I run into times when forgiveness is required of me. It is truly humbling to think that, as my husband stated in earlier chapters, you are truly called by God to be a "distributor of forgiveness."

I have always heard it said that the best gift you can give someone is a fresh start. That starting gate has a sign posted above it—*forgiveness*.

We all have our war stories. The things we have been through in our lives that have made us the people and the families that we have become. Our family is no different. Even in the middle of Brian writing this book, the warfare has been so intense. It seemed every "skeleton in the closet," every hurt, every offense, just kept creeping up trying to haunt us, or maybe assault us would be a better word. But we daily must *make a conscious decision* to forgive.

The devil doesn't want the message of forgiveness to reach the lost and hurting. The devil wants the message of "I will never forgive you" to be the loudest voice in your world. But no matter what satan's plans are, the only true voice has spoken from the cross, *"Father, forgive them; for they know not what they do"* (Luke 23:34). That voice is the voice of truth that cannot be silenced but must be proclaimed by us as believers.

I love the following quote from Corrie Ten Boom, a Christian woman who survived a Nazi concentration camp during the Holocaust. She said, "Forgiveness is to set a prisoner free, and to realize the prisoner was you."

## My Deliverance

I will never forget a very special day of deliverance for me personally. I had held a secret inside my heart for many years. At the time, I felt there was no way to fix the mess

I had made. I had released and forgiven everyone involved except myself. I was in the church praying alone one morning, and I can remember the Lord stopping me right in my tracks and He spoke these words. "Fear not, stand still, and see the salvation of your God. For the enemy you see today you will see no more forever." Truth was revealed to me that day. Knowing that the word He spoke to me was found in the Book of Exodus, I began to read it, and revelation for my breakthrough was released.

*And Moses said unto the people, Fear ye not, stand still, and see the salvation of the Lord, which He will shew to you to day: for the Egyptians whom ye have seen to day, ye shall see them again no more for ever* (Exodus 14:13).

I realized that day that I had an Egyptian that was chasing me, and God had called him "my enemy." I had been haunted, chased, and tormented by this enemy, all along knowing that I was saved and forgiven by Jesus. How could he have had the power to wear me out?

The key to my deliverance was to be found in the story of the word God had spoken to me that day. We have all read the story of the parting of the Red Sea many times. God told Moses to tell His people to "go forward." Believe me, you can move when God says move. He will not be stopped, and He will back up His Word to you just as He did for Moses. With the lifting of the rod, the Red Sea parted, and over a million people crossed on dry land. But that is not the end of the story. Let's read on.

*And the Egyptians pursued, and went in after them to the midst of the sea, even all Pharaoh's horses, his chariots, and his horsemen. And it came to pass, that in the morning watch the Lord looked unto the host of the Egyptians through the pillar of fire and of the cloud, and troubled the host of the Egyptians, and took off their chariot wheels, that they drave them heavily: so that the Egyptians said, Let us flee from the face of Israel; for the Lord fighteth for them against the Egyptians. And the Lord said unto Moses, Stretch out thine hand over the sea, that the waters may come again upon the Egyptians, upon their chariots, and upon their horsemen. And Moses stretched forth his hand over the sea, and the sea returned to his strength when the morning appeared; and the Egyptians fled against it; and the Lord overthrew the Egyptians in the midst of the sea. And the waters returned, and covered the chariots, and the horsemen, and all the host of Pharaoh that came into the sea after them; there remained not so much as one of them* (Exodus 14:23-28).

While they were in the process of moving forward, there was an enemy in hot pursuit. They walked across on dry land, but their deliverance was not complete until Moses stretched out his hand again to cause waters to return and drown the enemy. You see, we have been given an authority not just to part the Red Sea of difficulties in our lives, but we have been given the authority to shut the back door.

My enemy that had been chasing me was unforgiveness. I had not forgiven myself for the actions that had brought shame to me and my family. I prayed that day, released myself, and can say with all that is within me "the enemy that I saw that day has chased me no more forever." I was free from the tormenting thoughts, the regrets, the condemnation, the fear that had wreaked havoc in my mind and my emotions.

As I was typing a lot of the material you have read in this book, I came across something I found very interesting. Every time I would type the word "unforgiveness," I would get the little red, squiggly line that alerts me of a spelling error. I found it amazing that my computer did not recognize "unforgiveness" as a word. I actually had to add it to my computer's dictionary. That is the way our hearts should be. Just as the hard drive in my computer didn't recognize the word, it should not be found on the hard drive of our hearts. If it is found there, we need to immediately hit the delete button and erase that file once and for all. We have all heard the saying for years, "Christians aren't perfect, just forgiven." That's another one of those sayings that sounds great, but will take making a "conscious decision" to walk out in our lives.

By making this decision, I am not saying that the power of forgiveness is a license for you or others to sin. I am not saying that forgiveness is condoning someone's behavior. When we choose to forgive, we aren't saying, "What you did to me or someone else is OK." What forgiveness says to me is this, *"Your actions are God's to deal with, not for me to deal with."*

I believe that the power of forgiveness is the fuel that keeps our hearts burning with the desire to not just chase God but to go after the lost in the world. *Forgiveness isn't always the easy thing to do, but it is always the right thing to do.* Have you ever thought about how easy it is to minister to someone who is walking through a situation you didn't know about, you weren't involved in, nor did you know any of the parties that were involved? We always seem to have so much more compassion to minister to them. But that same compassion should be shown to those who have done us wrong. We need to lay down our lives for even those who have hurt us or done us wrong, not to mention those who have spoken against us. This is the ruler that we have to use to measure the degree of forgiveness we are walking in today. Don't fall short. Let's stretch out our hearts again. Shut the door, drown the enemy, let's walk in the place where the Egyptian of unforgiveness that has chased us, we will see no more forever.

*Appendix A*

# PRAYER FOR SALVATION AND HEALING

*I make a conscious decision to forgive every person who has ever hurt me, manipulated me, controlled me, or done me wrong. I forgive myself for any wrong decisions or actions that I have done. I forgive God for any time I feel my prayers weren't answered or He hasn't been there for me. I let the past go. I believe that Jesus is the Son of God and that He came to earth in the flesh. I believe that He died for my sins, shed His blood on the cross, and that God raised Him from the dead so that I could be saved. Jesus, forgive me for my sins and come into my heart and be my Lord and Savior. In Jesus' Name, I now confess that I am saved and I am born again.*

(I encourage you to immediately follow up with water baptism and become active in a local Bible-believing church.)

*Appendix B*

# SCRIPTURES ON FORGIVENESS

*And forgive us our debts, as we forgive our debtors. And lead us not into temptation, but deliver us from evil: for Thine is the kingdom, and the power, and the glory, for ever. Amen. For if ye forgive men their trespasses, your heavenly Father will also forgive you: but if ye forgive not men their trespasses, neither will your Father forgive your trespasses* (Matthew 6:12-15).

*For whether is easier, to say, Thy sins be forgiven thee; or to say, Arise, and walk? But that ye may know that the Son of man hath power on earth to forgive sins, (then saith He to the sick of the palsy,) Arise, take up thy bed, and go unto thine house* (Matthew 9:5-6).

*Wherefore I say unto you, All manner of sin and blasphemy shall be forgiven unto men: but the blasphemy against the Holy Ghost shall not be forgiven unto men. And whosoever speaketh a word against the Son of man, it shall be forgiven him: but whosoever speaketh against the Holy Ghost, it shall not be forgiven him, neither in this world, neither in the world to come* (Matthew 12:31-32).

*Then came Peter to Him, and said, Lord, how oft shall my brother sin against me, and I forgive him? till seven times? Jesus saith unto him, I say not unto thee, Until seven times: but, Until seventy times seven* (Matthew 18:21-22).

*Shouldest not thou also have had compassion on thy fellowservant, even as I had pity on thee? And his lord was wroth, and delivered him to the tormentors, till he should pay all that was due unto him. So likewise shall My heavenly Father do also unto you, if ye from your hearts forgive not every one his brother their trespasses* (Matthew 18:33-35).

*Why doth this man thus speak blasphemies? who can forgive sins but God only?* (Mark 2:7)

*That seeing they may see, and not perceive; and hearing they may hear, and not understand; lest at any time they should be converted, and their sins should be forgiven them* (Mark 4:12).

*Therefore I say unto you, What things soever ye desire, when ye pray, believe that ye receive them, and ye shall have them. And when ye stand praying, forgive, if ye have ought against any: that your Father also which is in heaven may forgive you your trespasses. But if ye do not forgive, neither will your Father which is in heaven forgive your trespasses* (Mark 11:24-26).

*Judge not, and ye shall not be judged: condemn not, and ye shall not be condemned: forgive, and ye shall be forgiven* (Luke 6:37).

*And Jesus answering said unto him, Simon, I have somewhat to say unto thee. And he saith, Master, say on. There was a certain creditor which had two debtors: the one owed five hundred pence, and the other fifty. And when they had nothing to pay, he frankly forgave them both. Tell Me therefore, which of them will love him most? Simon answered and said, I suppose that he, to whom he forgave most. And He said unto him, Thou hast rightly judged* (Luke 7:40-43).

*Wherefore I say unto thee, Her sins, which are many, are forgiven; for she loved much: but to whom little is forgiven, the same loveth little. And He said unto her, Thy sins are forgiven* (Luke 7:47-48).

*Take heed to yourselves: If thy brother trespass against thee, rebuke him; and if he repent, forgive him. And if he trespass against thee seven times in a day, and seven times in a day turn again to thee, saying, I repent; thou shalt forgive him* (Luke 17:3-4).

*Then said Jesus, Father, forgive them; for they know not what they do. And they parted His raiment, and cast lots* (Luke 23:34).

*Saying, Blessed are they whose iniquities are forgiven, and whose sins are covered* (Romans 4:7).

*So that contrariwise ye ought rather to forgive him, and comfort him, lest perhaps such a one should be swallowed up with overmuch sorrow* (2 Corinthians 2:7).

*To whom ye forgive any thing, I forgive also: for if I forgave any thing, to whom I forgave it, for your sakes forgave I it in the person of Christ; lest Satan should get an advantage of us: for we are not ignorant of his devices* (2 Corinthians 2:10-11).

*And be ye kind one to another, tenderhearted, forgiving one another, even as God for Christ's sake hath forgiven you* (Ephesians 4:32).

*And you, being dead in your sins and the uncircumcision of your flesh, hath He quickened together with Him, having forgiven you all trespasses; blotting out the handwriting of ordinances that was against us, which was contrary to us, and took it out of the way, nailing it to His cross; and having spoiled principalities and powers, He made a shew of them openly, triumphing over them in it* (Colossians 2:13-15).

*Is any sick among you? let him call for the elders of the church; and let them pray over him, anointing him with oil in the name of the Lord: and the prayer of faith shall save the sick, and the Lord shall raise him up; and if he have committed sins, they shall be forgiven him. Confess your faults one to another, and pray one for another, that ye may be healed. The effectual fervent prayer of a righteous man availeth much* (James 5:14-16).

*If we confess our sins, He is faithful and just to forgive us our sins, and to cleanse us from all unrighteousness* (1 John 1:9).

*He that saith he is in the light, and hateth his brother, is in darkness even until now. He that loveth his brother abideth in the light, and there is none occasion of stumbling in him. But he that hateth his brother is in darkness, and walketh in darkness, and knoweth not whither he goeth, because that darkness hath blinded his eyes* (1 John 2:9-11).

# About Dr. Brian Adams

Dr. Brian Adams is the pastor of THE ROCK located in Jackson, Ohio. Brian's passion is to challenge believers to "dare to believe" and to bring the Gospel to as many souls as possible globally. His testimony takes him from being a drug dealer to undercover narcotic officer to full-time preacher. He ministers strongly in the areas of healing and deliverance, bringing believers back to the truth that God still heals today. Brian travels globally and recently appeared as a guest on Sid Roth's *It's Supernatural!* television program. His unique style of preaching is accompanied with tremendous anointing for winning the lost and offering hope and healing to the hurting. His ministry focuses on the authority of the Gospel and the power of God to transform lives.

www.brianadamsministries.com
www.therockfgc.org
Brian Adams Ministries
PO Box 188, Jackson, OH 45640
740-286-3924 or toll free 866-386-3924
Email address: drbrian@brianadamsministries.com

# DESTINY IMAGE PUBLISHERS, INC.

*"Promoting Inspired Lives."*

## VISIT OUR NEW SITE HOME AT
## WWW.DESTINYIMAGE.COM

---

## FREE SUBSCRIPTION TO DI NEWSLETTER

Receive free unpublished articles by top DI authors, exclusive
discounts, and free downloads from our best and newest books.
**Visit www.destinyimage.com to subscribe.**

---

Write to:     Destiny Image
              P.O. Box 310
              Shippensburg, PA 17257-0310

Call:         1-800-722-6774

Email:        orders@destinyimage.com

For a complete list of our titles or to place an order
online, visit www.destinyimage.com.

FIND US ON FACEBOOK OR FOLLOW US ON TWITTER.

www.facebook.com/destinyimage      facebook
www.twitter.com/destinyimage       twitter